CONTRIBUTIONS TO INDIVIDUAL PSYCHOLOGY

Selected Papers by
Bernard H. Shulman, M.D.

ALFRED ADLER INSTITUTE
OF CHICAGO

Copyright © 1973 by Bernard H. Shulman, M.D.

Second printing 1977
Third printing 1981

Library of Congress Catalog Card No. 73-82047

ISBN 0-918560-18-7

Table of Contents

A COMPARISON OF ALLPORT'S AND THE ADLERIAN CONCEPTS OF LIFE STYLE:
Contributions to a Psychology of the Self *

Allport's Position

Gordon Allport and Alfred Adler have been previously compared by Ansbacher (1) and by Long (2) and found to be similar in their holistic approach to understanding man. Both Allport and Adler were found to consider man as purposive, future oriented, goal striving, and self-directing.

In a more recent work (3) Allport asked the question: Is the concept of *Self* necessary in psychology? He discusses the controversy between "psychology with a soul" and "psychology without a soul" and points out that in recent years the notion of *self* has been expressed in American psychology in terms such as "self-image," "self-actualization," "ego-involvement," etc. Allport points out that this new tendency to return to the ego is the result of the failure of positivistic analysis to satisfactorily explain personality. However, he warns, "the tendency to employ 'self' or 'ego' as a *factotum* to repair the ravages of positivism may do more harm than good." (p. 38) Allport then goes on to say a possible clue to the solution, so far as psychology is concerned, lies in a statement made by Alfred Adler, "What is frequently labeled 'the ego' is nothing more than the style of the individual." (4) "Life-style to Adler had a deep and important meaning. He is saying that if psychology could give us a full and complete account of Life-style it would automatically include all phenomena now referred somewhat vaguely to a self or an ego . . . would discover all of the activities and all of the interrelations in life, which are now either neglected or consigned to an ego that looks suspiciously like a homunculus." (p. 39) Allport distinguishes between what is *important* to a person and what is merely a matter *of fact* to him (what is central

Reprinted from *Individual Psychologist*, 1965, 3, 14-21.

and what is peripheral to his *being*). He adds, "All the regions of life that we regard as peculiarly ours . . . I suggest we call the proprium." He then composes *proprium* (pp. 41-53) of bodily sense, self-identity, ego-enhancement, ego-extension, rational agent, self-image (including present self-image and idealized self-image) propriate strivings, and the knower.

Allport concludes, "Once again we refer to Adler's contention that an adequate psychology of the life-style would . . . dispense with the need for a separate psychology of the ego. I believe Adler's position, though unelaborated, is essentially the same as the one here advocated." (p. 55)

In view of these comments, it seems appropriate to re-examine Adler's theory of the Life Style. This discussion will do so from three points of view: What Adler's theory was, how other individual psychologists have extended Adler's theories and the relationship between the Life Style and Allport's *proprium*. The paper will conclude with some implications for psychotherapy.

Adler's Theory of the Life Style

The most orderly presentation of Adler's views is to be found in the Ansbachers' excellent collation of his writings. (5) Their views follow here:

In 1907 (p. 30) Adler, while still a member of Freud's group, used the term "confluence of drives" and "transformation of drives." The latter term represented an idea which became important in Freudian psychology, but "in Adler merely foreshadowed his view that all causal factors, including drives, are relative to the individual's style of life." (p. 31) The confluence of several drives then provided a "main axis" for personality development. This concept was ultimately developed by Adler into the concept of "style of life." The Ansbachers point out (p. 95) that Adler introduced the term "guiding self-ideal" in 1912. This self-ideal (which Ansbacher carefully distinguishes from Freud's "ego-ideal") was the "fictional final goal" of the individual, the *causa finalis* of the mental life and its governing principles. (p. 95) "The fictional abstract ideal is the point of origin for the formation and differentiation of the given psychological resources into preparatory attitudes, readiness and character traits. The individual then wears the character traits demanded by the fictional goal, just as the character mask (*persona*) of the ancient actor had to fit the finale of the tragedy." (p. 94)

It was not until the 1930's that Adler developed the concept of Life Style in the sense that Allport uses. At this time (1933) Adler finally settled on the term "The Unique Law of Movement" which underlies the "Style of Life." (p. 174) The Ansbachers describe the various terms Adler used as equivalents of Life Style (self, individuality, method of facing problems, opinion about oneself and the problems of life, whole attitude toward life, self-consistent unity, etc.); and select from Adler's writings passages which describe Life Style as having the following characteristics:

1. It originates in the creative power of the individual who is trying to develop a rule of thumb for facing life.

2. It is self-consistent. It is coherent and unified and always follows the *private* logic of the individual.[1]

3. It is constant. It does not change from time to time or situation to situation. What remains flexible is the ability to find new and better ways of striving toward the goal inherent in the existing life style.

4. It is formed in early childhood. Both Adler and Freud considered childhood years very important — Freud, because certain events mold the child; Adler, because the child is forming at this time, his subjective opinions about life, his apperceptive tendencies and is creating his "guiding point" (self ideal). (5, p. 95) Once formed, the life style becomes increasingly harder to change, since it is constantly reinforced by the individual's selective apperception of life experiences.

---

[1] "Private logic" is a term used to denote the personal convictions and value systems of an individual by which he judges how to think, feel and act about events. Private logic may, but seldom does, follow the rules of formal logic, or of "common logic"; i.e., common sense. If one understands the private logic of a person, one understands his motivations and may predict much of his behavior.

5. It is sovereign. By means of selective perception, cognition, memory, etc., it presses the individual into a characteristic mode of living, a characteristic attitudinal position. It is a self-created construct which begins as a rule of thumb but is then elevated to the status of a law (the "unique law of movement").

6. It becomes the intervening variable between cause and effect, between the stimulation from the outside world and the responsive behavior of the individual ("soft determinism").

Later Additions

The concept of Life Style was examined by Dreikurs (6) who distinguished between a "life-style" and "life-plan." The "plan" consists of the basic concepts of the individual which set his attitudes and provide his frames of reference. The "style" is his characteristic *direction of movement.* According to this formulation the "fictional final goal" would be part of the life plan and both plan and style would be included in the term "unique law of movement."

For Mosak (7) the life style is a *set of convictions* which he separates into four component parts or aspects for teaching purposes and indicates that one can break it down into a greater of lesser number of components if one wishes.[2] These aspects are:

1. A self-concept

2. A self-ideal, which is like Horney's idealized self. (9) It includes all the individual wants to be and thinks he "should" be: his hopes, aspirations and goals. This seems to be Adler's "guiding self-ideal" (5, p. 95)

3. An environmental evaluation; convictions about life, people and the physical universe

4. Ethical convictions (which may not coincide with those of society); ideas of right and wrong, good and bad, etc., for *propriate behavior only.*

---

[2] The terms self-concept, environmental evaluation and ethical attitudes used by Mosak, are taken from Coleman. (8)

Aspects #2 and #4 share the "shoulds." Mosak separates them because #4 implies the existence of a moral sense, while #2 need not and he finds this a more convenient way of establishing a basis for teaching that the *feeling of guilt* is a *variety of inferiority feeling.* Inferiority feelings are seen as consequences of a discrepancy between convictions. The larger the gap between the self-concept and self-ideal, for example, the greater the feeling of inferiority (similar to Horney's description of the gap between self-concept and idealized image). (9) The inferiority feeling leads to compensatory conclusions and goals which may be further included in the self-ideal or which can be considered a fifth aspect of life style; namely, the "fictional final goal."

Mosak (10) specifically excludes from the life style nonpropriate activities and convictions. This type of distinction is the same that Allport makes between matters of *importance* to the individual and *matters of fact,* between what is vital and central and what is peripheral. In this respect, the whole question of life-style must be considered in the framework of a psychology of *values* as has been done by Mosak and Shulman. (10)

Shulman (10) describes the life style as developing according to rubric: "I am thus, the world is so, life demands such and such, therefore . . . " The self-concept plus environmental evaluation lead thus to the formation of a plan which includes a goal or end-point (wherein it is perceived that adaptaion will be successful) and a choice of action (which is perceived as leading toward the desired goal). Also, the self-chosen fictive goal will guide the individual toward those private ethics which will most help him to reach his private goal.

The attitudes in the life style can also be categorized according to the type of conviction (what the conviction is concerned with). Thus, the life style is a set of convictions dealing with Zarathustra's eternally recurring questions, "Why, wherefore, whither and how." The individual seeks answers to the questions: What am I?, What are my chances?, What is life?, What is important?, What must I do?, What does it all mean?, etc.

The life style can be understood as both the way in which the individual poses these questions (e.g. what he chooses to focus on) and how he answers them in his living.

Sicher and Dreikurs, however, reserve the term "life style" for the characteristic movement (i.e., one has the life style of a "beggar," a "prince," a "tyrant," etc.) for the *leitmotif* of the individual's behavior. Dreikurs points out that individuals with similar self-concepts, ethical values and ideas about life may still have different life styles; by which he means different characteristic *modi vivendi*.[3] Mosak and Shulman obviously use the term "life style" in a broader sense, including in it approximately all those aspects of personality that Allport would call propriate and all the various definitions used by Adler in discussing "life style."

Ferguson points out that Adler's theory of the Life Style requires at least four basic propositions. She lists these as:

1. The objective environment to which man adapts and with which he interacts is primarily a social environment.

2. The individual is a unit, an irreducible whole.

3. An individual develops a dominant motivation. The directive aspect of motivation is a goal. The dominant direction of the individual is toward this goal.

4. Within the limits of the objective environment, these "inner directive processes" serve as a "subjective environment" which provides direction and stimuli for behavior.

The concept of a "unified personality" together with that of "inner directedness" indicates the "main theme" and dominant motivating "goals" of the personality are based upon subjectivity perceived values.[13]

Adler saw all life as "movement," all "movement" as directed toward a goal which is evolved from the subjective environment. The basic motivation was the striving nature of life; life was growth, a movement from minus to plus. In humans this striving takes social form. If the striver has

---

[3] Personal communication to the author.

a sense of *gemeinschaftsgefuhl* (feeling of communality, social interest) his chosen goals will be pro-social. To the extent that his feeling of communality is stunted, the individual develops feelings of personal inferiority. The Law of Compensation (5, p. 97) leads the individual to choose fictive compensatory goals (guiding self-ideals) which would, according to the individual's subjective frame of reference, seem to effectively compensate for the inferiority. For each individual, the "goal" was his chosen way of fulfilling the basic motivation, his form of "upward striving." (11) Consequently, the main or dominant "goal" of the movement (or behavior) has several characteristics:

1. It is a fiction. It is *created* out of a subjective frame of reference and is a useful construct which enables the individual to direct his life according to his subjective values.[4]

2. It is private and individual rather than consensual and commonly held. (The question of cultural influences on private goals has not yet been clarified enough for us to include it in this discussion.) It is unconscious and not subject to consensual validation. Therefore, it does not follow common-sense, but the private logic of the individual.

3. It is causative in a finalistic sense. It exerts the directional pull of "telos" on behavior and values. This type of causation can be considered "internal causation."

4. It is a director or direction-setter. Movement in life has many possible directions. The goal limits the possibilities by excluding some and enhancing others. Therefore, the goal operates in one sense by limiting possibilities. "The goal of the mental life becomes its governing principle, its *causa finalis*. Here we have the root of the unity of the personality, the individuality. It does not matter what the source of its energies may have been. Not their origin but their end, their ultimate goal, constitutes their individual character." (5, p. 94)

---

[4] cf. Vaihinger's *Philosophy of As If* which influenced Adler's conceptualizations.

5. It is social in nature. The unique Law of Movement is developed to facilitate social adaptation, even though it may paradoxically interfere with this adaptation by reason of mistaken subjective precepts. Consequently, the goal can always be seen as a social goal.

6. It is necessary. Unless behavior followed some blueprint it would all be random behavior. The higher complexity of the human nervous system requires a cognitive blueprint, a plan, for meeting the subjective demands of life; the instinctual blueprint, which sufficed for lower animals, is no longer enough. It is also subjectively experienced as necessary and thus has an urgent and imperative quality.

7. It is adaptive. The final goal of adaptation underlies all the *basic psychic* strivings.

Comparison with Allport's Proprium

A. *Bodily sense.* This first aspect of the proprium is for Allport, an "anchor" for self-awareness. This term seems to have the connotation of physiological reference points which become part of an individual's body image. The *bodily sense* fits into Adlerian theory with ease. It is the individual's sense of "What is me," and thus a part of his *self-concept.*

B. *Self-identity.* This is not the equivalent of the term *self-concept* as used by Mosak and Shulman. (10) It is the "Who am I" (self-image). (See F below.)

C. *Ego-enhancement.* Allport describes this as the "unabashed self-seeking" trait of the personality. This idea resembles Adler's description of the upward striving of the human being. This idea has also been discussed by Van Dusen, (12) who finds in Adler the idea that the individual's personal goal is enhancement through "standing Forth"; what Adler called "striving for significance." The "Law of Compensation" in Adler's theories would also be an example of this. For Individual Psychologists, healthy ego-enhancement is achieved through *Gemeinschaftsgefuhl*, through constructive identification with the group (feeling of belonging).

D. Ego-extension refers to people, objects or ideals that are important to us. Such extensions in Adlerian psychology would be developed because they lessen personal feelings of inferiority; that is, they have an ego-enhancing quality. They are measured by the individual in terms of "What enhances me?" "What is mine?" "What is on my side?"

E. *Rational Agent* refers to the problem-solving function of the life-style. It is concerned with finding solutions, with methods of operation. Without this function, man could not develop a system of personal private logic which would enable him to bring a cognitive order into his world.

F. *Self-image.* The Adlerian self-concept would include bodily sense, self-identity and part of the self-image. Allport divides the self-image into 1) the way the patient regards his present abilities, status, etc. (What I am) and 2) his aspirations for himself (What I should be). It is the first part that would be included in the Adlerian *self-concept* while the *aspirations* would be included in the self-ideal. Allport says "the ideal self-image is the imaginative aspect of the proprium, and whether accurate or distorted, attainable or unattainable, it plots a course by which such propriate movement is guided." (p. 47) Thus, aspirations are direction-setters of behavior.

G. *Propriate striving.* Allport points out that a psychology of motivation based on impulses and drives and tension reduction seems adequate to psychologists accustomed to working with animals. He then adds that as soon as personality enters the stage of ego-extensions and develops a self-image, we are forced to postulate propriate strivings as motives (cf. Ferguson's basic proposition #4); Adlerians would say that since personality *is* social, its motives *are* propriate strivings. In this sense, propriate movement strives toward the fictional final goal and makes for unification of the personality. This is exactly the way that Adlerians consider that unity of the personality comes about: through the final *goal* which provides the *unique law* of movement. " . . . for Adler the self-ideal or fictional goal was the unifying principle of personality . . . " (5, p. 95)

H. *The knower:* the "cogniter,"; that aspect of the self which "transcends all the other functions of the proprium and holds them in view." (p. 51) For Adlerians this aspect of the self is the "decision maker" and the "believer." Dreikurs indicates that when each individual chooses a course of action he basically acts not according to *logic* but according to *psycho-logic,* that is, according to his own *biased apperception* of the world around him, and his place in it. (6) The *knower* is therefore always biased with regard to his own final goal and his convictions about himself. It is also the *knower* with the help of the *rational agent* who in psychotherapy can recognize his own bias (understand his own life style). The act of recognition implies a change in the knower and leads to further changes in the subjective convictions which constitute the proprium.

Implications for Psychotherapy

The more inappropriate and dereistic the chosen life goal, the more life becomes difficult and unpleasant, because the individual is not free to abandon the goal. The more narrow the life style, the smaller the probability of successful adaptive functioning within its limits, the more limited the modi operandi, the fewer the available modes of action, the more frequent the times of difficulty, the greater the possibility of decompensation (psychological bankruptcy).

The concept of life style as a governing system offers a new way of looking at the transaction called psychotherapy. The therapist, in his encounter with the patient, becomes an intruder, someone who tries to insert a foreign body into the cognitive-perceptual system of the patient. Psychotherapy, from this point of view, takes on the aspect of a potential struggle between the consensual logic of the therapist and the private logic of the patient, the latter being forced to defend himself because this scheme and this mode of being are all he knows or has experience of.

Such a concept also permits an ontological definition of the term *freedom.* The individual develops the life style because he needs a blueprint for living and adapting; having adopted one particular pattern, he is now limited by it. " . . . the free creative power of the individual in his earliest childhood, and his restricted power in later life, when the child has already

adopted a fixed law of movement for his life . . . " (12, p. 12)
Life style thus permits certain behavior but prohibits others.
It is a *limiter* because it is a governor. Freedom now becomes
the freedom to change, to transcend the governor, to modify
or discard the old pattern and find new ones, to make new
choices and test new possibilities, to change the accustomed
frame and find new reference points. This kind of *freedom*
becomes a desired goal in psychotherapy.

REFERENCES

1. ANSBACHER, H. "Causality and Indeterminism According to Alfred Adler and Some Current American Personality Theories." *Indiv. Psychol. Bull.* 1951, 9, 96-107.

2. LONG, L., M.K. "Alfred Adler and Gordon W. Allport: A Comparison on Certain Topics in Personality Theory." *Am. J. of Indiv. Psychol.* 1952-3, 10, 43-54.

3. ALLPORT, G. W. *Becoming.* New Haven, Yale, Univ. Press. 1955.

4. ADLER, A. "The Fundamental Views of I.P." *Int. J. of Indiv. Psychol.* 1935, 1,5-8.

5. ANSBACHER, H. & ANSBACHER, R. *The Individual Psychology of Alfred Adler,* N.Y. Basic Books, 1956.

6. DREIKURS, RUDOLF. *Fundamentals of Adlerian Psychology,* Alfred Adler Institute, 1953.

7. MOSAK, H. H. "The Psychological Attitude in Rehabilitation." *Amer. Arch. Rehabil. Ther.* 1954, 2, 9-10.

8. COLEMAN, J. C. *Abnormal Psychology and Modern Life,* Chicago, Scott, Foresman, 1950.

9. HORNEY, K. *Neurosis and Human Growth,* London, Routledge and Kegan, Paul, 1951. Chap. 1.

10. MOSAK, H. & SHULMAN, B. *Introductory Individual Psychology, A Syllabus, Chicago,* Alfred Adler Inst., 1961.

11. ADLER A. *Social Interest. A Challenge to Mankind,* New York, Putnam & Sons, 1964.

12. VAN DUSEN, W. "The Ontology of Adlerian Psychodynamics," *J. Indiv. Psychol.* 1959, 15, 143-156.

13. FERGUSON, E. D. Unpublished Mss.

LIFE STYLE*

What Is the Life Style

What Is the Life Style

Central to the concepts of Adlerian psychology is the Life Style concept. Adler started developing this concept at least as early as 1907 (1) but did not express it in its final form until 1933. (2) At this time he defined it as "the Unique Law of Movement" of the individual. The personality of the individual was seen by Adler as a unity and all drives, strivings, tendencies and aspirations were part of this unity and all inclined in the direction dictated by the unique law of movement.

Why It Develops — a biological overview

Some animals are instinctually programmed to such an extent that little decision making is left to the organism itself. The more complete the programming, the less is creative action required. Higher vertebrates are incompletely programmed animals. Instinctual patterns do not inform humans how to cope with the multitude of stimuli and challenges posed by a human life. The human is rather equipped with an ability to program himself through learning. Such an ability requires extended development of cognitive functions and as expected, self-programming type functions such as decision making, value setting, comparing and concluding are most highly developed in those animals who have the greatest cognitive abilities.

Rules are necessary for coping behavior. Where rules are not provided by instincts, they must be developed by other means. Rules are generalizations which permit the application of learned material to coping behavior. Without rules,

---

* I am indebted to Harold H. Mosak for assistance with some of the formulations in this paper.

16

each situation would require trial and error behavior. Even the primitive pleasure principle of Freudian psychology is a rule for determining behavior. The Life Style is the "rule of rules" for the individual. It is the cognitive blueprint for behavior which is required when there is no instinctual blueprint. But the Life Style is not merely a collection of rules, it is the organization of all rules into a *pattern* which dominates not only the rules but all coping activity.

How It Develops

Equipped with inherited receptors, processors, organizers and effectors; born into the human *Umwelt* with its particular perceptual world and its numerous possibilities for extension; even before its nervous system is mature enough to permit full locomotion, the infant's learning begins. The learning starts out by trial and error of the simplest variety as the infant tries to organize his world in order to cope with it. He locates, recognizes, compares, contrasts, times, sizes, tests, retests, and otherwise applies methods of learning until he develops rules which permit him to relate to the world in a less chaotic way. He studies cause and effect, good and bad, pleasant and unpleasant, desirable and undesirable until he is able to make primitive abstractions. These early rules continue to be developed and organized into an increasingly elaborate *pattern* which acts as an integrator for the rules. This early pattern is a rule of thumb. It is constantly reinforced as the child grows until the rule of thumb is elevated to the status of a law, the "unique law of movement." It cannot help but be reinforced by experience because it is the rule by which experience is perceived. Since it is a unique personal law, it receives all of the person's loyalties, as do the other familiar objects of early childhood. Since it seems to permit better coping it becomes as a private religion or personal myth. Since it is based upon a private logic, it is not influenced by common sense when that sense conflicts with the private logic.

Eventually the *pattern* becomes a dominant directive in the life of the individual, a cherished Holy Writ which propounds what is required by life and how it is best achieved.

17

Life Style as a "Cause" of Behavior

In most scientific discussion, the word cause is used in the sense of Aristotle's *causa efficiens;* namely, cause that is the "source of change or rest." Adlerians have also used Aristotle's concept of *causa finalis* when they discuss the goal directedness of behavior and the purpose of symptoms. This approach is frankly teleological and Dreikurs has even called Adlerians "teleoanalysts." The general concept of *cause* is a larger one however and the concept of *causality* itself leads us to speak of cause from more than one point of view. (5)

One type of cause discussed by Aristotle is the *causa formalis;* namely, the ordering or patterning of relationships that leads to specific results. It is in this sense that the Life Style is a "cause" of behavior. In what ways does it act as a determiner? It is 1) a limiter in the sense that any law limits, 2) It is a governor in the sense of a director of the overall line of movement, but 3) it is also a governor in the sense of a feed-back which reinforces or inhibits the movement.

The "law" which limits is based upon what Adlerians call *private logic*, the significant personal values and convictions which are not necessarily consensually validated. The *private logic* of an individual shows his own personal bias. Thus, every Life Style is biased. The Adlerians, however, do not condemn bias uniformly; instead they consider it necessary for functioning in the world. Not all decisions which life requires can be made according to logic because logic does not provide answers for all situations.[1] Some decisions must be made according to an alogical system; the personal bias of the individual who can choose a course of action on

---

[1] e.g. Choosing a mate or even deciding to marry does not work well if one tries to choose by logic. If men used logic they would never marry at all. Emotional bias is required many times or we would not decide which way to move.

the basis of prejudices, emotional evaluations, etc.[2] Although we have described the Life Style as a limiter, Adlerian psychology considers that a person always has the ability to change the Life Style and thus transcend the limits. In this sense the Life Style as *cause* is a "soft determiner" rather than a rigid one and behavior is not inevitably determined but based upon a series of choices which delimits direction of movement. The Life Style is transcended through the educative experience of psychotherapy or sometimes through life experiences which lead to self-awareness and recognition of subjective truths which we may call "conversion" experiences.

The Components of the Life Style

If we consider the life style a pattern, then perhaps we can recognize the recurrent themes in the life of each individual that can convey to us the essence of the *individual* pattern. Where, however, we examine a great many individual themes we find that they cluster around a few main elements. This is not surprising. If the Life Style is intended as a basic adaptive pattern, then the main elements will deal with some of the very basic issues in every human life. Since these basic issues are viewed through the subjective eye of the self, one can expect to find that the Life Style speaks about these issues in expressed or implied *convictions* about them. Indeed, one way of recognizing the components of the Life Style is to identify the convictions expressed by it and to try to classify the convictions according to the kinds of issues they are concerned with. The issues seem quite basic: the meaning of life, sentiments about human relationships, an evaluation of the self and what life requires. The expressed convictions are reducible to platitudes. This is partly

---

2 Where we are able to solve a problem in life by logic we do not, by reason of the Law of Parsimony, bother to become emotional about it. If we cannot solve it by logic we work ourselves into a passion in order to solve it that way. This is why human beings have the strongest emotional reactions concerning those issues that make no logical sense and are most vehement when they cannot successfully support their arguments with logic.

because a platitude is an effective if unsophisticated way of expressing a subjectively perceived truth and partly because these convictions are formed at a time of life when simple generalization is one of the few intellectual devices available to the person. In addition, it is the purpose of the Life Style to simplify — that is, to provide easily apprehended rules for behavior and naturally, oversimplification is a common result. Indeed oversimplification, exaggeration of one aspect of life at the expense of others and mistaking a part for the whole are three main mistakes in logic that can be found in a study of Life Styles.

The convictions which we identify as components of the Life Style are convictions about "what is," conclusions about behavior and ideals. Each of these can be broken down into parts:

1. Convictions about "what is"

    a. The self-concept — this set of convictions express the person's deepest feelings about himself and include his various subjective views of the different aspects of himself. It includes:

        (1) The body sense, — "what is me." Allport uses this term in his discussion of the *proprium* (3. p. 41) and describes it as an "anchor" for self-awareness. There are a number of physical and physiological reference points that everyone uses to identify what is crucially himself and not something else. Thus, excreta, nail parings, etc. are not ordinarily identified as a part of one's own body, while teeth are. Certain physiological processes are considered to be taking place in the body (ex: digestion) while others (heart beat) are ordinarily thought of as "actions" of the body. Convictions about the integrity of the body and its basic adequacy fall in this category.

        (2) Self-identity — "who am I." According to Adlerian theory, the development of identity takes place in a social field. Other people are therefore the reference points for this part of the self-concept and it is intricately connected to the convictions about the environment which will be discussed subsequently.

20

The "who am I" question is part of a social and cosmic *location* which each person tries to identify for himself. Thus, "I am me, I am not one of them"; etc. refers to a basic recognition of the self as a distinct entity. I am male, not female; I am young, not old; I am Catholic, not Protestant, are all ways of locating the self through reference points.

(3) Self-image — "what am I." It may seem hairsplitting to distinguish "what am I" from "who am I" since both deal with identity. But identity is more than one thing and the self-image is not a *location* of the self among referents but an *evaluation* of the self, actually of one's worth or value. Thus, the self-image includes value laden convictions: "I am not masculine enough," "I am not pretty enough," "I am not smart enough," "I am an innocent victim," "I am evil," "I am good," "I am inadequate," "I am doomed to failure," "I am special," "I am entitled," "I am something precious," "I am of little use" are all common examples of self-images. Thus, the the self-image speaks about abilities and status and assigns worth. It can even include convictions about one's potential; such as, "I will never amount to anything," or "If only I were properly loved I would be able to cope with life."

Some self-concepts are absolute, that is, no matter what conditions exist the self-concept does not change (e.g. "I am no good — now — in the past — and always, is an example of an absolute self-image). More usually, it is the body sense and self-identity that are more absolute. The self-image itself seems more contingent upon other factors; thus, "I am worthwhile if someone loves me" is a contingent or relative self-image which depends upon a factor outside the person. Perhaps the self-image seems less absolute to us because we are clincians and therefore in the business of trying to change destructive and inappropriate self-images and less concerned with body sense and self-identity.

b. The environmental evaluation or World Image — is a set of convictions about all items (objects, processes and locations) outside of the subjective self, and to the whole concept of "outside" in general. It is the "outside" with which we are generally coping. (Sometimes we have to cope with the self). Not all aspects of the "outside" are of equal importance; some can be safely ignored, others are seen as necessary to the self. Thus: for some people a flight of birds across the sky has no personal significance, for others it is an omen. Also, a parent figure is often of great personal importance; an unknown human being has little meaning to most of us.

The World Image includes:

(1) The image of the physical cosmos — Life Styles frequently contain statements about the nature of life in the world. A common such statement is "Life is unpredictable." Life can also be seen as surprising, predestined, immutable, chaotic, orderly, accidental, directed by powerful forces, malevolent or a place where "all's for the best."

(2) The image of the social world — People can be seen as friendly, supportive, competitors, inferiors, directing powers, open or closed to communication, hostile, rejecting, uncaring, confusing, unpredictable and so on. Their approval and/or love and/or attention may be seen as necessities. Sometimes all human relations are seen as untrustworthy; often the different sexes are assigned different qualities. One person may feel unable to influence others in any way or may see others as operating according to arbitrary whims. Another may believe that people can be successfully appeased if one is always "good" or never makes a "mistake."

2. Ideals

a. The significant issues of life — This aspect of the Life Style answers the questions, "What is important," "What is desirable," "What is undesirable." Proponents of "natural law" have been wont to say that animals follow two primary urges; the urge to self-preservation and the urge to preservation of the species. Adlerians would certainly agree that such urges exist but the Life Style is the final arbiter of what is important and these two supposedly immutable and primal urges often operate in distorted ways or not at all. Self-preservation often comes to mean preservation of one's "face" rather than preservation of life (cf. *hari-kari* — a form of self-immolation to preserve honor). Preservation of the species has usually been an ideal rather than a goal. The goal has more often been preservation of the group with which one most closely identifies (perhaps the family). In almost every description of a Life Style can be found the selected ideals that the particular person will value above others. One person will value prestige above all else, a second will value money, a third will make "love" his first choice, a fourth will value safety above all.

One corollary of this point of view is that it considers basic ethical attitudes to be much more an individual psychological matter rather than a result of mass propaganda or social system. The way in which culture influences Life Style will be discussed later.

b. Moral judgments — Basically, the ideals state the conviction that *a* is important while *b* is not, and that *c* is desirable (good) while *d* is not (bad). However, sets of ideals almost always offer a *moral judgment* about life and for the self; namely, how life and the self "should" be. (This is the aspect of the Life Style that can be compared to the super-ego of psychoanalytic theory). Thus: "I should never sin," "I should never act cowardly," "I should always be right" are idealized demands upon the self, while "People should always play fair," "God shouldn't have let it happen" and "They should stop persecuting me" are all idealized demands upon the environment.

3. The Conclusions about behavior

It is our purpose to explain the Life Style and we have tried to do so by logic and analogy, by example and metaphor. We have given it one definition as a set of rules or laws. It is in the conclusions about behavior, as expressed in the life style, that one can perhaps see most clearly how it is a set of rules. We have called this aspect of the Life Style "conclusions" but they are, like the other aspects, apparent to us as "convictions." We call this one "conclusions" for another reason. It is because one way we have of describing the Life Style is to say that it seems to fit into a rubric: "I am . . . , Life is . . . , therefore . . . The conclusions about behavior are the "therefores."

a. The goal — "what to do" — Adler called this item "the final fictive goal"; meaning, the end point of the striving determined by the life style. He also called it the "guiding self-ideal." In accordance with the Law of Compensation (4, p. 79) the goal is the *chosen* way of fulfilling basic psychological motivations. He also called it the "dominant goal" to signify that it dominates the psychic strivings and therefore the individual's life. The Life Style, which we have also called the "Unique Law of Movement" is always movement toward the goal; yet, the goal itself is the nexus of the Life Style and the pattern swirls around it and tends toward it. The Life Style is organized around the goal and this concept leads to the Adlerian concept of "Unity of Personality." The goal itself is the unifier, the pattern is the organization of the uniting process.

The goal, like the other aspects of the Life Style, is a fiction. It is *created* out of a subjective frame of reference and enables the individual to direct his movement toward it. It is also private and individual rather than consensual. It is unconscious and not subject to consensual validation. It is causative in a finalistic or teleological sense as the Life Style is causative in a formal sense. It is Aristotle's *causa finalis*. As Adler says, "The goal of the mental life becomes its governing principle, its *causa finalis*. Here we have the root of the unity of the personality, of the individuality. It does not matter what the source of its energies may have been. Not their origin but their *end,* their ultimate goal, constitutes their individual character." (4, p. 94)

Of course, the goal is adaptive. In Adlerian theory, the final goal of adaptation underlies all the basic psychic

24

strivings. Furthermore, the goal can always be seen as a social goal; that is, it never is able to ignore the social field in which man lives. The language the Adlerian uses to describe someone's dominant goal always has referents to others. Perhaps this only betrays the Adlerian's own brainwashed way of thinking, but that is the way it always seems to come out.

Typical examples of dominant goals are: "I want to be first, to be on top" (overambition). "I want others to protect me and run interference for me" (dependency). "I want to never lose control." "I want to be the center."

A typical example of a Life Style can then be written according to the aforementioned rubric:

> I am small and weak
> Life is dangerous
> Therefore others must protect me

Adlerians have a penchant for describing Life Styles in a word or phrase and would say that this is the Life Style of a "weak baby."

Another example is:
I am the rightful heir to my father's power.
Life is here to appreciate me and serve me.
Therefore, I have to be the center of attention.

We would call this the Life Style of a "crown prince."

b. The methods — "how to do it" — The rubric we have devised does not specifically include all aspects of the Life Style and is really a shorthand way of expressing the Life Style. One could easily add a statement about methods. Many techniques of behavior change during a person's life. He learns new ones and discards old ones as his understanding and experience grows and he refines his techniques. It is not these methods that we mean here, but only those methods that consistently throughout the life history of the person are used as behavioral

25

techniques for striving toward the dominant goal. Common methods can be clearly seen in those clinical syndromes we call the personality pattern disorders. Thus, the schizoid personality uses a method we call "distance-keeping," the inadequate personality uses one we call "failing," and so on. Each dominant goal may have one or more methods commonly found in association with it and similar methods may be found associated with disparate goals.

Thus:

"I want to be first, to be on top"
  Possible methods:
  "I will impress everyone with my power"
  "I will be the best in everything"
  "If I can't be the best, I'll be the worst"

Or: "I want others to protect me"
  Possible methods:
  "I will charm them into loving me"
  "I will display my weakness and win sympathy"
  "I will only associate with those who protect me"

Long-continued patterns of behavior are often "methods" in our sense. The short phrase names that Adlerians use for Life Styles often describe the method as much as the goal; e.g., "weak baby" and "crown prince" are ways of describing a set of attitudinal responses to life. If we say one has the Life Style of a "victim," we are saying something about the method he uses to achieve his goals as well as trying to tell the "gist" of his whole pattern in one analogical phrase.

Influences on the Life Style
A developing set of concepts can be subject to many influences, more during its early plastic stages than its later rigid ones. If one could map the whole developmental history of a Life Style one would see at work the effects of body constitution, culture and perhaps pure chance as well. Several of these influences deserve more extensive mention.

1. Ecological factors — I had at one time thought that the very act of being human would limit the variety of Life Styles we would find among humans. It seemed natural to assume that humans would not have Life Styles suitable for dogs or horses. On closer thought, I was obviously wrong; the Life Styles of some people are perhaps more suitable to animals than humans. I suspect there is another connection between Life Styles and the general biological factor of ecology. Just as "nature" devises animals and plants to fit all but the most extreme situations, so is there a tendency for the variety of Life Styles to accommodate itself to all of the available social living spaces (or social roles). The effects of the available social roles upon the developing Life Style will be seen more clearly in the discussion of the family constellation.

2. Constitutional factors

   a. Genetic factors — whether or not there is direct genetic influence upon the Life Style has not yet been conclusively answered, but no observable genetic effects appear in the Life Styles we have found. For the present our answer must be that the Life Style is behavior of an order that cannot be measured directly for genetic factor influence.

   b. Constitution — by the same token, the effects on Life Style of endocrine glands, the central nervous system, etc. cannot be directly measured except in the case of obvious physical or mental defect. Unless a child is severely feeble-minded, he will develop a life-style if only he lives long enough. Otherwise, intelligence seems to be a factor in influencing the Life Style in the sense that intelligence is a tool for coping behavior and the ability to cope depends partly on the tools one uses.

   Constitution also influences in the following way: A very pretty girl will receive different reactions from her environment than a plain one. The same is true for a very handsome boy. A strong, muscular, athletic child will find certain opportunities that are closed to his less adept counterpart. Also, the quick-witted child will see alternatives the duller child misses. But in all these factors, it is the response of the social situation to the constitutional "given" that determines how much the constitutional trait will influence the Life Style. And, of course, it is never the trait itself, but the way in which it is used in the interaction with life.

c. Physical defects — According to the theory of organ inferiority and the Law of Psychic Compensation, defects can influence the development of the Life Style whenever something is subjectively perceived as an inferiority; it requires that some way be found of minimizing the defect or detouring around it, so that it does not interfere with coping behavior in life. Therefore, if a child is born with an observable defect, acquires one during his development or fancies that he has a deficiency; this becomes a "fact," a "given" of his life to which he must make some answer. Thus, King Richard says, "Since I cannot be a lover, I'll prove a villain" (8). As always, the answer he makes is his own creation.

3. Developmental factors — psychoanalytic theory assigns specific psychosexual periods of development to the child and believes that personality is formed partly on the basis of how the environment reacts to the child during these periods. Psychoanalytic theory also uses an energy model rather than a general systems model, so that unless one can measure how much a particular id drive was frustrated for how long a period of time there is no applicability to the theory except in terms of hindsight. Erickson, of course, has tried to expand the psychoanalytic model into a social model. Sullivan also tried to build a social developmental model in terms of the psychosexual stages which he renamed "zones of interaction."

From the Adlerian point of view, all these efforts seem naive attempts to force a Procrustean order upon the developing child. All other things being equal, the child is weaned, toilet-trained, walks and talks sometime during the course of his development. He even becomes aware of sexual feelings; but the adults personality has never depended upon the technique of toilet training nor upon an oedipal *kerygma*.

That there are critical periods for the development of certain traits is beyond question. Liddell's experiments have demonstrated the critical period for development of social traits in certain animals. Furthermore, certain human skills require practice from an early age or they cannot be well learned at all.

Nevertheless, the information that would be given to us by a better understanding of the developmental factors should be closely paralleled by the information given us by an understanding of cultural and familial factors. Perhaps even better than developmental factors they will tell us what situations the child found and what answers he gave.

4. Cultural factors

Culture is seen by Adlerians as both a limiter and expander of the psychic life. Culture provides certain basic ways of looking at the world and therefore encourages certain tendencies in the development of the Life Style. A culture which stresses individual enterprise and accomplishment will encourage different behavior from one which stresses conformity to tradition. Moreover, the values assigned to sex, age, socioeconomic status, skin color, place of birth, etc. will all be influenced by the culture and will influence the growing child's picture of the world around him and his role in it. Culture can limit, in the sense that it helps train the individual to perceive in *some* ways. Culture therefore provides a measuring stick for the growing child to use in evaluating his world and a frame of reference for his ideals and goals.

5. Family influences — the family constellation

Each child is born into a certain specific condition of life. It includes his ordinal position, who and what are the other family members, his sex and his physical make-up. During the course of his life this specific condition may change; other sibs may be born, parents may die, crippling illness may come and so on. His parents may be permissive, strict, overprotective, rejecting, demanding, pampering, inconsistent, etc. They are nevertheless models for the child. The family atmosphere may be oppressive or free, harmonious or full of conflict, warm and close or cold and distant, clear and simple or confusing and contradictory. Family standards may demand high performance and family myths may promise severe punishment for the child who fails to live up to the expectations.

Each child responds to the situation he finds according to his subjective perceptions. The environment in turn responds to the activity of the child, feeding back to him the data he uses to further refine his rules of operation. The pattern of interaction is what the Adlerian calls a "family constellation": a grouping of members playing various social roles in relation to each other. Family constellation is considered an important influence on the developing life style, but at the same time, the investigation of the family constellation is an important technic the Adlerian uses to diagnose the life style.

The main elements of the family constellation for Adlerians include:

a. Ordinal Position — There are 5 basic ordinal positions in Adlerian psychology and all other positions are combinations of the five. The positions are "psychological" more than "chronological," e.g., a first-born may be dethroned and may play the role of a middle child while the second-born by virtue of overrunning the first actually plays the first-born role.

Each of the 5 positions has a characteristic "situation" attached to it and in the life style of each person can often be seen his response to the situation of his particular ordinal position. Such a concern with ordinal position often seems picayune, but it is not. I have seen a trained Adlerian correctly identify the ordinal position of 80% of the people in a room by observing casual behavior. Furthermore, I have done the same myself, even to my own surprise. Obviously, the Adlerian is recognizing something that is characteristic.

The 5 positions and their associated "situations" are:

(1) Only child — he never had a rival and other people are curiosities rather than competitors. However, he may never have learned to share.

(2) First born child — he once had it all to himself and would still like to be first and foremost.

(3) Second child — he started late and has to catch up.

(4) Middle child — he is surrounded and squeezed. He feels in danger of losing his portion.

(5) Youngest child — the trail is well broken and he is never dethroned. He also has a great deal of ground to overcome.

b. Sibling allies and rivals — A sibling is not only a member of the same family, he is a fellow inhabitant of the psychological space within the family. He wants the attention of the same parents, fights for the same territory and possessions and otherwise is a fact of life. Siblings relate to each other along ecological lines. The relationship may be that between competitors, co-operators, distance-keepers ("you go your way and I'll go mine"), dominance and submission, and other complementary forms of behavior. A relationship between siblings of disparate age may be almost like that of a parent and a child. According to Adlerian theory, the sibling closest in age, is usually the fiercest competitor. Competition, however, is not always shown by open conflict, it is more often shown by diverse paths and interests. How many times has a mother said, "My 2 boys are as different as night and day. You wouldn't think they came from the same family?" But, this situation is actually the norm. The first born of one family will be much more often like any other first born than he will be like his next younger sib.

There are certain common external factors which influence sib relationships. One of these is parental favoritism. Being a favorite gives a sibling an added feeling of security in his place. A second is sex. The particular family values and myths regarding the place and function of each sex will strongly influence the way brothers and sisters will relate to each other. It must also be understood that some sibs are "special." The crippled sib and the retarded sib are examples. They occupy a special ecological niche and are often excused from the competition. On the other hand, if they occupy a good deal of the mother's time, they can be seen as oppressive tax-gatherers by the other sibs. The dead sib does not lose his entire place in the family. He often becomes an ideal against which the other sibs are measured.

c. Parent-Child interaction — Adlerian theory warns specifically against several kinds of parental behavior which discourage the child from developing effective attitudes toward life. These are overprotection and overindulgence which prevent the child from learning to take responsibility for himself; rejection, which discourages the child about his worth; excessive standards, which discourages the child about his ability; inconsistent discipline which leads the child to feel that life is arbitrary and unpredictable and authoritarian behavior which leads the child to feel that he depends upon the power and opinions of others for his place and must either placate the powers or defeat them.

Karen Horney (6, p. 490) has devised a list of the six social needs of the developing self to which Adlerians would add a 7th. These 6 are:

(1) emotional warmth
(2) security
(3) freedom
(4) good will
(5) guidance
(6) healthy friction

The added (7) is a feeling of worth.

The child responds to the parental behavior as one of the "givens" in its world and seeks to come to terms with it. Sometimes he chooses only to rebel against it because he considers it impossible or self-defeating to submit to it. Whatever happens, it influences the developing Life Style.

d. Models (Parents, older sibs and other adults — Parents not only interact with the child, they provide models (as do other significant adults and older sibs). The function of the model is to display varieties of behavior to the child who thus learns various techniques of behavior and their consequences. How men behave, how women behave, how adults relate to each other, how they meet crises, what they consider important, what they consider proper all are displayed to the view of the child who chooses what he will imitate and what he will reject. If the models display a narrow or distorted range of behavior the child has little opportunity to learn alternatives and tries to use the little he has learned to deal with his situation. Thus, a first-born son with an indulgent and submissive mother and a dictatorial tyrannical father is very likely to become a rebellious dictatorial child himself, demanding the mother's submission and constantly enraging the father who then punishes the child and further teaches him to be arrogant, demanding and interested in power.

e. Family Atmosphere — Each family tends to have an atmosphere of its own which grows out of the relationships and values of the family and which is itself influenced by intercurrent events and the position of the family in the outside world. Some families live in harmony, others in conflict. In some families the members are in conflict with each other at all times except when an outside danger threatens. Some families have a democratic, some an autocratic and others an anarchic atmosphere. Sometimes family members are close to each other, sometimes distant. They may help each other or ignore each other. In some, the atmosphere is confusing or contradictory or secretive or hostile or gloomy and despondent. Initiative may be encouraged or discouraged. The overall theme may be tragic, comic or dramatic. Oppressive standards may hang like a cloud over the family so that everyone feels like a failure.

The disorganization of a family — by death, divorce, etc. affects the atmosphere. Children who are "survivors" of dead siblings, who are orphans, who have lost a parent early by divorce, who have lived with chronically ill or emotionally disturbed parents show the consequences in their Life Styles which may reveal the courage the child used to face the issue or the discouragement which left him feeling helpless to better his lot.

f. Family Values — The values of the models are not always openly expressed but become clear to the child through his interaction with the models. Indeed, the actual stated values may be at variance from the real values and ideals of the models. The family values all represent ideals and therefore demands upon the child. In some families good human relations may be a value, in others material gain. Intellectual accomplishment, social prestige, propriety, morality, rugged masculinity, polite behavior, are all examples of common family values. Some values are sex-linked; i.e., men are supposed to be strong and silent while women are supposed to be emotional and talkative.

If the pressure to live up to the values is intense and if the values seem excessive to the child, he finds himself *oppressed* by the values and reacts by rebellion, surface submission and inner rebellion, rationalization and other devices for dealing with an oppressive demand. Nevertheless, the child must respond to each family value that he perceives as applying to him. He may accept and try to fulfill or may reject the value and may choose from among the thousands of techniques that human beings have developed to deal with their own ideals those which seem to help him preserve his sense of worth in the face of the ideal.

g. Roles available — The family is an ecological unit. The values and atmosphere define the available ecological niches in the family. One small patch of prairie can hold many different species of animals provided they do not intrude upon each other too much. The same is true of the family. A family may have room for one good student, one helpful domestic girl, one black sheep son, etc. If a second child tries to also be a good student, or mother's favorite, or whatever, he intrudes upon a sib's territory and conflict ensues which all too often does not satisfy anyone. The role of black sheep is sometimes one of the most satisfying roles in the family. It is a dramatic attention-getter; a way of being impressive and important in the family and the choice of this role by a sibling usually means that he is extremely ambitious to impress and has discovered that misbehavior (and perhaps retaliation) are suitable for this purpose. Some roles are available to more than one sibling. For example, it is usually possible for a family to have more than one black sheep. At other times, however, one sibling may so outshine the others in some way that the others give up and do not compete in this area at all. Some roles are more available to one sex than the other. One child may be the unselfish, generous and cheerful one; his sib may be the bossy, critical achiever. The roles complement each other and therefore do not lead to significant conflict.

Thus are available roles determined and constructed and they are perhaps the most impressive example of the creativity of the child as he builds his life.

Functions of the Life Style

We have already described the Life Style as the cognitive blueprint, the "rule of rules" and the "unique Law of Movement" for each individual. We have discussed the Life Style as the "formal cause" of behavior, as a governor and feedback. However, we can define with more precision the functions of the Life Style as we see them in operation in each person.

1. The organizing and simplifying function — as previously stated, the Life Style provides a set of rules by which values can be assigned, a hierarchy can be established priorities determined. Thus, it lends an overall organization to psychic activity.

2. The selecting function — this is actually a six fold function. Selecting occurs in:

a. direction-setting — the Life Style evokes a certain line of movement as the person grows and matures. The line of movement can be deduced from a historical inquiry into the person's life, but the themes of the movement can be seen in the Life Style. Thus, the person who must avoid failure may avoid all those situations in which he has no guarantee of success. The ideals of the life style thus become beacons for the line of movement.

b. selective perceiving — events are perceived according to the Life Style, that is according to a private logic. If the Life Style states that "I am weak and impotent," then I perceive myself so and will act accordingly.

c. guiding action — As a person who feels weak and impotent I will most likely find myself unable to act effectively in many situations. Instead, I will be passive and/or turn to others for help. I will not see opportunities for aggressive action because I will not be looking for them.

d. predicting and anticipating — I will anticipate failure if I try aggressive problem-solving. Should an opportunity for aggressive behavior present itself, I will not behave so because I will not believe such a course of action will be successful.

e. the radar function — The Life Style not only permits predicting and anticipating events, it also keeps a watchful eye out for special situations. If the Life Style says that one must be cautious and avoid danger, then the signals of danger can be watched for by a constant alert — an early warning radar system which gives ample warning. Conversely, if we meet another person who will fit into our desired *schema* and permit us to play the role we wish, our ability to recognize such a person is part of the radar function. When the right person comes into our sight, the alert sounds and we can begin moving in.

f. the decision making function — many daily decisions are made on the basis of common sense. Where, however, common sense runs counter to the private logic of the Life Style, the latter prevails. The Life Style is based upon subjective, not objective considerations. Furthermore, there are some decisions that are often not made according to common sense because sufficient data is lacking. Common examples are decisions which will have unknown consequences in an uncertain future; namely, decisions which are a gamble, a chance. Choosing a mate is a situation which requires a willingness to take a chance. This type of decision is made according to private logic, that is, the logic of the Life Style.

3. The problem-solving function — In a broad sense, the Life Style is a set of directions for the general problem of coping, of adaptation. Life can be viewed as a succession of problems to be solved. For each person, it is the Life Style that sets down the guidelines for his own problem-solving.

4. The control of experiences — the selective perception of the Life Style permits an additional special kind of problem solving; namely, coping with the problem of evaluating and classifying experience. A so-called traumatic event becomes such because it is so designated by the Life Style. Actually, current and past experience are perceived according to the Life Style. Moreover, if my line of movement requires me to have a certain type of experience, I will arrange it. Thus, the distrustful person arranges to be betrayed, the pessimist arranges to fail in his endeavors, etc.

A classic funny story describes how the Life Style is used to control experience. A father had two sons, one an optimist and one a pessimist. In order to counter what he considered extreme points of view in his sons, the father, for Christmas, gave the pessimist a beautiful gold watch and the optimist a stocking filled with manure. On Christmas day he noticed his dour-faced pessimist son and asked, "What did Santa bring you?"

"Santa brought me a watch. I held it to my ear but it didn't tick so I threw it in the garbage."

At that moment, the other son came dancing into the room, shouting, "Daddy, Daddy, Santa brought me a pony, and I'm going outside to look for him."

5. The archeological function — this function permits us to use the earliest childhood recollections as a diagnostic device to determine the Life Style. Memory is selective in line with the Life Style and thus a person's **early life** is reconstructed in his memory as his Life Style dictates. He can find in his memory those events he considers formative and significant, the "causes" of his behavior, and so on.

6. The myth-making function — The Life Style is a myth and makes myths. The self-image and world image are mythical entities through which the person tries to organize his understanding of the "truths" of the world. The important issues of life are defined by the Life Style: what is the meaning of life, what is masculinity and femininity, what ethics govern behavior, and so on.

7. The reinforcing function — the Life Style guides the person toward having those experiences which tend to reinforce the style itself. If the Life Style says "Life is dangerous," the selectivity of the Life Style will lead the person to experiences that reinforce this view. Thus, the Life Style tends to become more fixed with advancing age as it is constantly reinforced by usage.

8. The self-protecting function — when events occur that would seem, objectively to call into question the Life Style itself, selective perception again intervenes to filter out, reconstruct or reinterpret the events so that they do not threaten the cherished set of rules. One cannot give up the set of rules one has until one has an alternative that is equally trustworthy. The process of reorientation in psychotherapy is largely a matter of replacing old convictions with better ones.

9. The self-related functions — Some life style functions are related to the self-concept and ideals which we have described as component parts of the life style.

   a. The self-defining function — the life style serves to identify and define the self, it's characteristics and its boundaries.

b. The self-viewing and judging function — one **perceives** and evaluates himself according to his life style. Satisfaction or dissatisfaction with the self is an evaluation dependent upon the values in the Life Style.

Basic Mistakes

We have already said that oversimplification, exaggeration and mistaking the part for the whole are three common mistakes in logic found in the life style. By what right do we presume to judge when a person has a mistaken style of life? Are we not always judging from our own bias? It is true that we are in danger of setting ourselves up as judges of what people should think and believe, but perhaps we can define a set of standards which are reasonable and commonly acceptable by which we can judge when a life style is mistaken. Some basic mistakes are easy to see, others are more subtle but all of them have certain characteristics which permit us to consider them mistakes. These characteristics have been described by Karen Horney (7, p. 133) and called by her the characteristics of "overdriven attitudes." It would seem to us that the term "basic mistake" is synonymous with Karen Horney's term. She has also described these characteristics as the identifying characteristic of "neurotic claims." According to her, an "overdriven attitude" can be recognized because it is:

(a) irrational
(b) insatiable
(c) impossible
(d) inappropriate
(e) intolerant
(f) wanted without effort
(g) egocentric
(h) vindictive
(i) compulsive

The basic mistakes are usually outside awareness. They often were more appropriate to the childhood situation than the current one. But the most obvious indicator of the basic mistake is probably the therapist's evaluation of "If he did not misinterpret life at such and such a point, he would not have the neurotic problems." Consequently, the defining of a basic mistake remains largely a matter of selection by the therapist. To overcome this difficulty, the authors are in the habit of using two diagnosticians rather than one to determine both life style and basic mistakes. (Two heads are more consensual than one).

The mistakes themselves can be categorized further:

1. Distorted attitudes about the self.
   Common examples are:
   a. I am less capable than others
   b. An evil spirit resides in me
   c. I cannot face any unpleasantness
   d. I am someone special and unique
   e. I am entitled to my own way
   f. I am unlovable, undesirable and unworthy
   g. I am an innocent victim

2. Distorted attitudes about the world and people.
   Common examples are:
   a. Life is completely unpredictable
   b. Life is a jungle (dangerous and frightening) or (dog eat dog)
   c. People are no damn good (Men are only out for one thing. Women are fickle).
   d. Life penalizes any mistake
   e. Life is too confusing
   f. Life offers me no opportunity (doesn't give me a chance)
   g. Life makes too many demands
   h. Life is unfair

3. Distorted goals. Some of these have already been mentioned. Others are:
   a. I must be without flaw (perfect)
   b. I must be more impressive than anyone else
   c. Everyone must love me
   d. I must be a "good guy"
   e. I must "get" as much as I can
   f. I must find perfect security
   g. I must never submit
   h. I must be one of the lions in the jungle
   i. I will have my revenge on life

4. Distorted methods of operation

Examples include:

a. Finding fault in order to elevate oneself
b. Excessive dependency
c. Excessive competitiveness
d. Relating to others in exploiting and manipulating ways
e. Distance keeping from others and life's requirements
f. Excusing oneself by blaming others, circumstances, etc. from responsibilities appropriate to the self
g. Antinomianism — self-deification
h. Excessive pride
i. Rebelling against all authority
j. Insistence on one's own way
k. Making mountains out of molehills
l. Putting all the eggs in one broken basket
m. Excessive self-indulgence
n. Taking the easiest course
o. Excessive self-control and caution. ("Nothing ventured, nothing lost").
p. Dishonesty (with self and others) including the distortion of logic to make it compatible with one's own wishes
q. Ignoring what one does not wish to confront
r. Vanity
s. Avoiding any initiative
t. Provoking life and others in order to feel justified

5. Distorted ideals

a. A "real" man is aggressive, fearless, heroic and never defeated
b. A "real" woman commands an entourage of men and receives gifts daily
c. The world will only be right when everyone's wishes are completely satisfied
d. I want a love deeper than the world has known before
e. Any transgression should be severely punished
f. The only thing worth being is a "star" (or genius). Nothing less is worth working for.

6. Distorted conclusions

This category partakes of the others but some of the distorted conclusions can best be mentioned separately.

a. Pessimism — nothing will work out right anyway (despair)
   (1) Life is just a trap
   (2) I am doomed to failure
   (3) One can have faith in nothing
   (4) I won't be able to endure it
   (5) There is no point in trying
   (6) I may as well live it up as long as I can. Any day the ax will fall
   (7) Before the ax falls I'll destroy as much as I can

b. X conquers all (solves all problems)
   (1) x=love
   (2) x=reason
   (3) x=money

c. Cynicism
   (1) Never give a sucker an even break
   (2) Everyone is only out for himself
   (3) It's never what you do, it's who you know
   (4) There's always an ulterior motive
   (5) It's all a conspiracy

d. Fanaticism
   (1) The other side is always wrong
   (2) This is the best of all possible systems
   (3) Discipline (repression) makes the world go 'round
   (4) I am the only one who has the "real" truth

The Clinical Uses of the Life Style

The Life Style is not only used as a diagnostic instrument; it also provides a valuable reference point in psychotherapy, counseling and guidance.

1. Diagnosis

a. The Life Style provides an overview of personality in several dimensions: The concept of the self, the view of the world, the basic motivations and the usual methods of operation.

b. Past events and current problems can be related to and understood in terms of the Life Style. Behavior can be understood in terms of the private logic of a person who is acting according to his own beliefs and anticipations.

c. The Life Style can be used to predict future behavior. It is not able to predict events but permits us to extrapolate future probabilities along those parameters that are issues in terms of the Life Style. A person with the Life Style of a "weak baby" will behave accordingly, even in his relationship to a therapist.

2. Treatment

a. Part of treatment consists of revealing the Life Style to the patient. One discusses it with him, explains some of the factors that led to it, describes the effect it would have on behavior, shows how it has led him to difficulties and exposes its internal logic and consistency.

b. The Life Style becomes a reference point for therapy. It presumes to show what is mistaken and what needs change. Interpretations of current and past behavior are made in terms of the Life Style and the memory of the past as well as future expectations are shown to be affected by the selective bias of the Life Style.

c. Basically, change in personality structure is considered to be a change in the Life Style. Thus, its various aspects become not only a reference point, but also a focal point for therapy which tries to change personality.

3. The Life Style can be used as a tool to assess the amount of personality change from therapy. It is a characteristic and repeated finding that the earliest childhood recollections change during successful psychotherapy, just as other perceptions of the past change.

Thus, the Life Style determination is an extremely valuable aid to research or change in psychotherapy, as well as a routine check to be used by the therapist himself for assessing the individual client.

Summary

The life style is a superordinate organizational pattern which directs behavior. By means of selective perception, cognition, memory, etc. it codifies rules for characteristic attitudinal positions. It becomes the intervening variable between efficient cause and effect, between the stimulation of the outside world and the responsive behavior of the person. It is formed in early childhood and is self-reinforcing through selectivity. It is a self-consistent, coherent, and unified. It is constant; it does not change from time to time or situation to situation, though it is not necessarily rigid. It can be recognized by its repeated appearance as a theme in the life history or even everyday behavior of an individual. It develops through trial and error and is influenced by physical, developmental, cultural, and familial factors. It is a necessary rule for coping behavior, to bring order into one's relationship with the challenging and confronting world. It is therefore of critical significance to the clinician who wishes to understand the "whys?" of human behavior.

REFERENCES

1. Adler, A. *Study of Organ Inferiority and its Psychical Compensation*. New York: Nervous and Mental Diseases Publishing Co., 1917 (translated from the German of 1907).

2. Adler, A. *Social Interest: A Challenge to Mankind*. New York: Putnam & Sons, 1964. (Translated from the German of 1933.)

3. Allport, G. W. *Becoming*. New Haven: Yale Univ. Press, 1955.

4. Ansbacher, H. ————, R. *The Individual Psychology of Alfred Adler*. New York: Basic Books, 1956.

5. Aristotle. Metaphysics. Book 5, Chapter 2.

6. Ford, D. H. & Urban, H. B. *Systems of Psychotherapy: A Comparative Study*. New York: Wiley, 1963.

7. Hall, C. S. & Lindzey, G. *Theories of Personality,* New York: Wiley, 1957.

8. Shakespeare, W. *Richard III,* Act. 1.

THE FAMILY CONSTELLATION
IN PERSONALITY DIAGNOSIS *

While the family constellation is generally recognized as important in personality development, in personality diagnosis it has been stressed mostly by Adlerians. Dreikurs has described it as:

A sociogram of the group at home during (the individual's) formative years. (It) reveals his field of early experiences, the circumstances under which he developed his personal perspectives and biases, his concepts and convictions about himself and others, his fundamental attitudes, and his own approaches to life, which are the basis for his personality (4, p. 109).

The writer has been using in practice and teaching a list of questions by Dreikurs (4, pp. 110-112), an interview guide which provides a bird's-eye view of the personality in its nascent state, permitting still to see "the child in man." Since students have frequently asked for elaboration regarding what one looks for in taking a family constellation and why, such elaboration is attempted in this present paper.

Underlying Assumptions

Several important assumptions regarding the dynamics of the formative years are made in Adlerian theory.

1. Personality is the result of *purposiveness,* of an active training on the part of the child; self-training — in traits he considers will be most useful to him. Without being aware of this, he will train "those qualities by which he hopes to achieve significance or even a degree of power and superiority

---

* Reprinted by permission from *Journal of Individual Psychology*, 1962, 18, 35-47

in the family constellation" (3). Not that he necessarily considers these traits ideal, but he must come to terms with his limitations. For example, a girl may most desire to be strong and masculine, but may recognize the impossibility of achieving such a goal. She may then decide to train herself in certain traits of submission because these would serve her best, although they may still be contemptible in her private value system.

2. Personality is formed in *social relatedness*, the family being the first social group of the child. "In his efforts to play a part in group life (within his first group, his family), the child is guided by the example of and his experiences with other members of the family. . . . The influence is dynamic and not mechanistic" (5, p. 5).

3. Personality is *phenomenologically determined*; that is, by the child's own perception of what he needs. In deciding what is needed, the child influences his future pattern of living, and may make the crucial mistakes that may later cripple his endeavors.

In summary, the purposive, socially related personality development depends on the child's perception of himself and others. His subsequent training takes place in line with the basic dynamic principle; namely, that man strives to move upward from a minus to a plus position.

Ordinal Position

Adler seems to have been the first psychologist to point to the ordinal position in the family as a personality determinant (1). Here it must be emphasized: (a) Like all determinants in Adler's view, it provides only probabilities since the individual's response is always a creative act of self-determination. (b) Ordinal position is not to be taken literally, but in its context. "It is not the child's number in the order of successive births which influences his character, but the *situation* into which he is born and the way in which he interprets it" (2, p. 377). If the eldest is feebleminded, the second may acquire the life style of an eldest child. If two children are born much later than the rest, the elder of these may develop like an eldest child.

Briefly, the various family positions have been described as follows. The *only child* is unique, he is weaker and smaller than his family, and need not share his prerogatives. The *eldest child* has been dethroned by a competitor but retains his position of being first. He thus will make an effort to remain first, unless he is surpassed, and becomes discouraged, then giving up the struggle and accepting a role secondary to his rival. The *second child* (and each succeeding child) finds himself in the position of starting a race with a handicap. Characteristically, he will feel the necessity to catch up to the rival who is ahead of him — again, unless he becomes discouraged. The *middle child* has neither the superior position of the eldest nor of the youngest. Characteristically, he feels squeezed, and either elbows his way to a more favorable spot, or is in danger of being squeezed out of competition. The *youngest child,* being last, may feel "not least" and try to overtake all the others. Or, if he is pampered, he may decide to remain a baby.

These are the five basic positions, and all others are variations, combinations, or permutations of these five. For example, a family of nine children may be divided into three groups of three. In a case where this actually occurred each child showed traits of his group and his position in the group; the patient was the 5th, or the middle child of the middle group and showed exaggerated middle-child characteristics.

The *favorite* has an undisputed place of prestige; he need struggle less to make his mark. He therefore conforms more easily and expects to be more acceptable than the other siblings. On the other hand, he may never learn to fight for his position, and may become unable to face a situation in which he is not the favorite. The *non-favored* sibling may learn early to accept "second-best," or to depend on himself, without feeling discouraged by lack of deference of others.

Parental Influences

It is a truism that parents exert a great influence on the child. They are his earliest and often his only models, from whom he chooses values, attitudes, and techniques. Parents are forces to be obeyed or defied, and models to be imitated or from which to turn away. Much of this takes place before the development of speech, without the child's awareness.

The parents' behavior generally sets the atmosphere of the home, i.e., whether it is peaceful or warlike; cheerful or depressing; marked by warmth, closeness and mutual involvement; or cold, distant and detached. The parents also encourage certain directions or behavior by allowing some of the children's techniques to be successful and others not. Some family values are common to the culture and can be found throughout the community, others vary from family to family.

Like ordinal position, parental influences by no means inevitably determine the child's behavior. "Nevertheless, children of the same family . . . show an inclination to similar behavior, developing characteristic values and moral concepts, especially when these are clearly defined and accepted by both parents" (5 p. 9). When the parents provide separate, or confused and contradictory examples, it is not easy for the child to decide what he is supposed to be. When there is marked conflict between the parents, one of the children may view this as a natural state of existence. He may take sides against one of the parents, or may decide to remove himself as much as possible from the conflict, and withdraw or disown the family.

The behavior of the child always reflects some facet of the parent's attitude and values, just as it reflects the child's own. One can assume that a power drunk child has at least one parent to whom force and forcefulness have a high positive or negative value. The child who fights his mother, has a mother who fights him. The child can be said to have "caught" from his mother the interest in opposing and in power.

If the grandparents were important, the child may choose to imitate one of them rather than a parent. If other persons live with the family "some of them may play a more important role for the patient's development than the parents" (4, p. 114). An extremely discouraged child may feel that he belongs only to his pet and companion, usually a dog.

Family Dynamics

Infinite patterning between siblings and parents is possible. A first-born may pattern himself after the parent perceived as having the more desirable position (when there is a sharp enough division between the positions of the parents); he may become convinced that he cannot match the atainments of the desirable parent, and yet fruitlessly continue to do so; or he may give up and switch to another form of behavior. The second child may choose to imitate the other parent or those aspects of the dominant parent that the first-born has overlooked. Divergence in behavior between siblings is partly due to competition between them for a place in the sun; the second avoids the territory of the first and goes elsewhere to seek his fortune.

According to Dreikurs, personality traits are the children's responses to the power politics within the family group. "Similarities and differences . . . indicate alliance and competition" (5, p. 11). "The siblings who are most alike are the allies" (4, p. 113). Conversely, the siblings most different from each other are the main competitors, even though there may have been no open rivalry.

Dreikurs distinguishes between rivalry and competition, describing the first as an open contest, the second as having "a much deeper impact on each child leading to the development of opposite character traits . . . as each child seeks success where the other one fails" (5, p. 10). Competition develops mainly with the proximal sibling, the one who always had to be taken into account during the formative years.

Siblings who died very young may have had considerable influence on the patient's life; they may be responsible for parental anxiety about the patient's health and survival or they may represent an unbeatable rival, since nobody can compete successfully with a dead brother or sister. Sometimes a patient may have felt accused or responsible for a sibling's death, so that his whole childhood life was affected (4, p. 112).

Sometimes a child will carry his opposition to another family member so far that he cannot freely choose what he wants, but must wait until he knows what the other wants, so that he can oppose him. Opposition may be in the form of overt defiance, negativism, passivity, or overt attempts to please the opponent while secretly arranging to disappoint him.

However, differences need not indicate competition. It may be that the parents encouraged different traits in the different children. Or, in a family with one boy and one girl, differences may reflect how each accepts his sex role.

Family Constellation Interview

To elicit information pertinent to the family constellation, Dreikurs, as mentioned initially, has devised an interview guide, following Adler's pattern, which is shown in essence in Table I.

Not all items of this guide are pertinent in any one case. They need not be followed in any special order, nor should they be asked mechanically. Indeed, the patient's answers will often suggest other, further questions. Although all the information can be gathered in one interview, if needed, it is usually advisable to go more slowly so that the patient may think about the family constellation. The total time required is at the most two hours.

An important advantage of this technique is that it is conducive to objectivity on the part of the patient, and a good way to get him to talk about significant people in his life. If he tends to guard himself, he may do so less with these specific questions which require specific answers, especially since he seldom knows what they might signify in the total personality picture. Furthermore, defensive covering up is brought to light if the answers are inconsistent. Even if the patient cannot answer all questions, he can, if he tries, answer enough of them to permit the formulation of his family constellation. Some patients become more cooperative when told that the questions, concerned with childhood behavior as they are, have no current "moral" value.

The ratings (see Table 2) are not all to be taken at face value. The siblings who try to please, for example, may alienate, because they try to please in order to exploit. The rebellious child may use overt or covert techniques; if the

50

patient cannot say who was most rebellious, ask, who got into most mischief. The most intelligent may not have gotten the best grades in school since good grades also imply willingness to work and cooperate. The hardest worker may not be the most helpful; he may work hard only on his own personal interests. The person whose behavior seems contradictory — conforming and rebellious, considerate and selfish — is a person of extremes, capable of using positive and negative, prosocial and antisocial ways of behaving according to whatever his perceptual system requires. He may conform if life pleases him, and rebel if it does not. It is not generally known that certain traits which are not in themselves inferior can still function as organ inferiorities. Extreme good looks and superior intelligence, for example, may cause disturbances in the child's social adjustment and call forth compensatory tendencies. A similar problem may be found in a wealthy child among poor children.

The ratings are intended to show how the siblings found their areas of success and failure. The ratings also give a profile of the patient's position on each of these continua. This helps to give an idea of his status evaluation of himself in relation to the other siblings and to show how consciously he feels inferior.

The present author has found the following additional questions useful: What is the father's occupation, the extent of his friendships and social participation, the time spent at home, his worldly success? A woman should always be asked if she ever wanted to be a boy, and about her reactions to the menarche and puberty. A man should be asked about doubts of his masculinity. One might ask about significant childhood illnesses, whether one sibling was excessively frail or sickly. Were there other stress situations such as a death of a parent or sibling, birth of a sibling, any drastic change in familial environment? It is pertinent to know the family's economic situation and whether the family was a member of a minority group in the neighborhood.

A Case

This case description follows the order of the Family Constellation Interview Guide (Table I). The patient, Pearl, is a woman of 35 years. Her sibling sequence was: Mary (plus 5 years), Jack (plus 3 years), the patient, Richard (minus 1 year).

A. *Description of Siblings:* Most different from Pearl was Richard, her chief competitor. He was active, aggressive, charming, wanted his own way. Pearl was more bashful and quiet. She was a good child and a good student, getting into little mischief. Mary, the eldest, was the bossiest, a forceful person who was also a good student. Jack was rebellious, fought with his father, and was not good in school. Note that Pearl's description, in answer to these open-ended questions, stresses the values of goodness, being good in school, and aggressiveness.

B. *Ratings of Personality Attributes:* Shown in Table 2.

C. *Sibling Interrelationships:* No one took care of any other. They all played together. Pearl got along best with Jack though she disapproved of his behavior. She could not feel close to Mary who was so critical. Neither did she feel close to Richard; perhaps she resented that Mother spoiled him.

D. *Description of Parents:* Father had an explosive temper, but has now become more mellow. He wants his own way and has strong ideas about how children should behave. He is a hard worker who tried to provide well for his children. Mary knew how to please him; they shared some intellectual interests. Pearl tried to please Father, but was afraid of him and could not feel close to him.

Mother was warm, could not hold a grudge, got stepped on by her friends, tried to please, was never strict, and seldom punished. Pearl was most like Mother. While Jack was like Father in temper, Mary was like him in seriousness and intellectual interests. Richard wanted his own way like Father.

Father was dominant, though he shared decisions with Mother. Mother thought Father was too hard on Jack, but Father couldn't stand being talked back to. They seldom quarreled, Mother usually tried to please Father. Father seemed more ambitious for the children.

Interpretation

Personality Development: The answers to the above questions give us the following picture: Pearl is the third of four children with an older sister and brother and a younger brother. The eldest, Mary, achieved a dominant role in the family and retained it through her assertiveness, conformity, intellectual achievements, and ability to please and persuade the parents, especially the dominant father. Jack, the second, apparently felt unable to compete with Mary on her chosen ground, and tried to assert himself in more forceful and negative ways. These tactics did not work, and Jack became increasingly discouraged, probably feeling he had no place at home and was more accepted among his friends. Whereas Mary was either willing to please the parents or win them over with persuasion, Jack only complained about them and opposed them. He, however, could feel successful outside the house by reason of his physical and mechanical prowess.

Pearl was impressed by Mary's success and Jack's failure. Therefore, she tended to imitate Mary and avoid displaying behavior that got Jack into trouble. However, not feeling able to achieve Mary's success, she stressed conforming and submissive traits, becoming most obedient, most helpful and most proper. This is a direction frequently chosen by the person who hopes that his "goodness" will win him a favored position. Pearl's choice of this direction was also influenced by the apparently unpleasant consequences of "badness' as seen in Jack.

Richard and his success as a carefree, selfish favorite discouraged Pearl. In spite of her virtue, she was not as successful as either Mary or Richard; she was "squeezed" between them and felt like a loser. Dreading the consequences of open rebellion and committed to "proper" behavior, she maintained an outer conformity while training herself to be sensitive and perceptive to unfairness. In her pessimism, her sensitivity became her chief tool of rebellion, and by her suffering and her virtue she felt elevated into the role of martyr.

Richard, as the youngest and mother's favorite, probably never felt the obligation to be virtuous as Pearl did. He used charm, sociability, and assertiveness to find his place, and seemed confident that he had a right to do as he pleased. He was successful where Jack had failed.

Thus, each child excelled in a different area: Mary in the intellectual area and in her ability to win respect; Jack in the so-called masculine area of physical prowess; Pearl in the area of idealism and virtuous behavior; and Richard in social leadership and doing as he pleased.

The guiding lines suggested to the children by the example of the parents were that women are expected to be good and helpful, while men are expected to want their own way. Mary somewhat imitated the dominant father; Jack used the father's own weapons of force and temper and got into a contest with him; Pearl avoided Jack's problem by becoming obedient; while Richard avoided it with charm. Both middle children were "squeezed" by the oldest and youngest, who found more successful techniques.

The patient imitated the good, sweet mother and equated femininity with goodness and submissiveness. She felt, however, that all her efforts got her nowhere, and she rebelled inwardly, through unhappiness and sensitivity.

Current Situation: The patient is married, a housewife, and the mother of an 11-year old son. The husband is a hard-working business man, moderately successful. She feels that the marital relationship is good, but wishes that her husband would give her more sympathy and support in her endeavors to influence the son. While her husband is protective of her, he is also critical of her attitude toward the son, saying, "boys will be boys." The son is a weak student, not helpful around the house, wants his own way and, though he can be charming, is often rude to his mother. She wants him to behave better, be a better student, and "love his mother more."

What light does the analysis of the family constellation throw on the patient's present situation? She came for treatment because she was suffering from a depressive reaction precipitated by difficulty in controlling her son. In an attempt to help her son more, she had consulted several child-guidance agencies. There her own role in her son's misbehavior was pointed out to her. Her sacrificing nature and desire to be good, which had previously given her self-esteem, now became faults. Instead of a good mother, she now felt herself a bad mother. Thus she became severely depressed and sought psychiatric help for herself.

She had always felt it was a difficult job to raise her son because he was so demanding. But partly, she expected trouble anyway, because she had acquired the belief that it was the lot of a woman to suffer and to sacrifice. Partly, she found her own sense of importance through being a sacrificer, and thus was not able to stop indulging the child. Furthermore, her son reminded her of her younger brother, Richard, who had generally done what he wanted and gotten his own way. Through being defiant, demanding, abusive and critical of her, her son reminded her also of her older brother, Jack.

The perfectionistic moral standards that she developed during childhood were still with her. She still felt she had to be "good" although she really did not expect her virtue to bring any reward other than that of martyrdom. However, she had thought of herself as a person who suffered in a good cause. Now, her role as a good person was threatened by the difficulties in her relationship with her son, and this threat was too much for her to bear. She could not face the idea that her son's difficulties might be caused by her failure. She responded by suffering from herself, becoming the chief victim of her own defect. As in her childhood, the patient saw no choice but to be virtuous and sit in judgment on the unfairness of life through her sensitivity and silent criticism. By being depressed and unhappy she was now atoning for her "badness" as a mother.

Psychotherapy with Pearl would include teaching her to see her mistaken use of sensitivity as a device for finding fault with life, and her mistaken idea that nothing she can do will offer her a chance to find a place. She needs to see that her over-concern with goodness has probably aggravated her son's provocative and defiant behavior; he "shows her up as a bad mother" perhaps in rebellion against her excessively high standards or propriety. She also needs to see that all her outward conformity conceals an inner rebellion and antagonism and that she too (like most depressed patients) wants her own way and silently loses her temper and sulks when her idealistic standards are not met.

Summary

Individual Psychologists see personality development as a purposive, socially related, phenomenologically determined process. They see the individual's family constellation as a most important environmental influence. A Family Constellation Interview Guide, questioning the subject about his parents and siblings, and calling for his rating of himself and his siblings in essential respects, is presented, discussed, and illustrated by a case. It reveals the subjectively perceived early environment and the individual's choice of reactions to it. It gives an historical illumination of the patient's present values and techniques, opinion of himself and others — in short, of his style of life — in less time and more easily than any other diagnostic tool with which the writer is acquainted.

REFERENCES

1. Adler, A. Individual-psychological education (1918). *In Practice and Theory of Individual Psychology.* Totowa, N.J.: Littlefield, Adams, 1959. Pp 317-326.

2. Ansbacher, H. & R. *The Individual Psychology of Alfred Adler.* New York: Basic Books, 1956.

3. Dreikurs, R. *Fundamentals of Adlerian Psychology.* Chicago: Alfred Adler Institute, 1953.

4. Dreikurs, R. *The psychological interview in medicine.* Amer. J. Indiv. Psychol. 1952-53, 10, 99-122.

5. Dreikurs, R. *Psychology in the classroom.* New York: Harper 1957.

TABLE I

Family Constellation Interview Guide

Sibling sequence: List all siblings in descending order, including the patient in his position. Give patient's age, and note for each sibling the plus or minus difference in years between him and patient. Include siblings now dead.

A. **Description of siblings:**
1. Who is most different from you? In what respect?
2. Who is most like you? In what respect?
3. What kind of child were you?
4. Describe the other siblings.

B. **Ratings of personality attributes:** Obtain a rating for each sibling, including the patient, for each of 21 attributes. Ask first for the extremes of each attribute and then, where the other sibs fit in. The 21 attributes are given, in essence in the left-hand column of Table 2, where they are shown with answers from an illustrative case.

C. **Sibling interrelationships:**
1. Who took care of whom?
2. Who played with whom?
3. Who got along best with whom?
4. Which two fought and argued the most?
5. Who was Father's favorite?
6. Who was Mother's favorite?

D. **Description of parents:**
1-2 How old is your Father? Mother?
3-4 What kind of person is your Father? Mother?
5-6 Which of the children is most like Father, and in what way? Mother?
7 What kind of relationship existed between your Father and Mother?
   (a) Who was dominant, made decisions, etc.?
   (b) Did they agree or disagree on methods of raising children?
   (c) Did they quarrel openly? About what? How did these quarrels end?
   (d) How did you feel about these quarrels? Whose side did you take?
8 Which of the parents was more ambitious for the children, and in what way?
9 Did any other persons (grandparent, uncle, aunt, roomer, etc.) live with the family? Describe them and your relationship to them.

57

TABLE II

Pearl's Ratings of Herself and Her Three Siblings Regarding the 21 Attributes of Section B of the Family Constellation Interview Guide (Table I)

Siblings in sequence, and their ages relative to patient's age

Attributes	Mary-plus-5 yrs.	Jack-plus-3 yrs.	Pearl	Richard -1 yr.
1. Intelligence		All seemed equally intelligent		
2. Work attitude	Hard worker	Preferred to take it easy	Hard worker	Can work hard when he wants to
3. School grades	Best grades	Poor grades	Good grades	Fair grades
4. Helping around house	Helped	Tried to avoid chores	Most helpful	Least helpful
5, 6. Conformity, rebellion	Generally conforming	Most rebellious toward Father, ran away from home several times	Most conforming	Did what he wanted and got away with it through his charm
7. Trying to please and its effectiveness	Pleased, because knew how to do what parents wanted	Only tried to please his friends	Tried to please the hardest but was less successful than Mary and Richard	Pleased the most because of charm
8. Criticism, judgmental attitudes	Openly critical of other siblings	Rebelled, but did not openly criticize	Often felt critical but did not voice this	Not critical
9, 10. Considerateness, selfishness		Selfish at home, not with friends	Most considerate	Most selfish
11. Having own way	Parents let her have her way, respecting her ability and judgment	Tried, but did not get his way, because he antagonized Father	Tried to obey rather than have own way	Had his way the most, could get away with things

58

12. Sensitivity, easily hurt	Not sensitive, the most persuasive arguer, would try to prove she was right	Belligerent and defensive, would argue he was unfairly treated	Most sensitive and easily hurt, would sulk and cry when she felt unappreciated	Happy-go-lucky
13. Temper tantrums		The only one with tantrums		
14. Sense of humor	A serious person	Good sense of humor	Always unhappy and tense, but covered it up	Good sense of humor
15, 16. Idealism, materialism	Practical, yet idealistic	Materialistic	Most idealistic	Materialistic, always wanted more
17. Standards, aspirations (for achievement, behavior, morals, etc.)	Highest intellectual achievement and ambitions	Seemed unambitious and with lowest standards	Highest moral standards, most interested in "proper" behavior	Low morals, but could get things done
18. Physical and sex-linked attributes	Not athletic, not so interested in her appearance, most assertive verbally	Best athlete, good at mechanical activities, strongest, good fighter, most masculine	Not athletic, not pretty, best dresser, most feminine, most shy	Best looking, good athlete
19. Maintaining friendships	Few but close friends	Many friends but Father did not like them	Some friends, tried to like everybody	Most friends, most popular, a leader and organizer socially aggressive
20, 21. Being parental favorite, reject	Father's favorite	Most punished by Father	Favorite of neither, felt closer to Mother	Most spoiled by Mother, Mother's favorite

AN ADLERIAN THEORY OF DREAMS

The discovery of REM, their use as an indicator of dreaming sleep and the characteristics of REM states have forced re-evaluation of the traditional theories of dream psychology. Modern dream theory probably begins less than 70 years ago with Freud's *Interpretation of Dreams*. Dream psychology became a popular subject for several decades and all of the major dissenters from Freud constructed their own theories to explain dream psychology, each explaining in what way his theories matched and differed from those of Freud.

A great part of Freud's early work in psychology including dream psychology, has always remained acceptable to Adlerians. In a 1936 paper (2), Adler honored Freud for "laying the foundation of the science of dream interpretation" and described what he considered Freud's valid contributions:

1. The demonstrations that emotional attitudes in the dream point to its actual meaning more than the figurative or verbal elements.[1]

2. That there is a distinction between manifest and latent content.

3. Dreams employ the same dynamisms used in slips of the tongue, daydreams and other waking behavior.

Wexberg, an important Adlerian writer in the 1920's, discusses in more detail the ways in which Adlerian dream theory follows Freud; namely, that it accepts the idea that dreams show hidden tendencies and personal conative patterns; that latent content indicates the real meaning; that dreams use condensation, displacement, distortion and representation by opposites; and that some dreams are wish fulfillment dreams. (15, 49)

Adler, however, disagreed with Freud's notion of the *censor,* which he called . . . "nothing else than the greater distance from reality that prevails in sleep." Adler means

---

[1] This is a rather general statement. Some dreams do not manifest emotional attitudes, verbal elements are missing from other dreams and the metaphorical element is sometimes the main key to understanding the dream, as Adler certainly indicates in other writings.

Reprinted from *Dream Psychology* and *The New Biology of Dreaming,* ed. by M. Kramer, C. C. Thomas, Springfield, Ill., 1969.

by this that dreamer uses autistic mental processes rather than socially learned and consensual ones. (4, 253) On the other hand, Adler claims that one function of the dream is *self-deception,* a concept certainly very close to Freud's *censor.*

Although it never seems to have been discussed in the literature, there are at least three points on which the Adlerian theory of dreams would agree with the theories of Carl Jung. The first point is that the dream, like any other psychic phenomenon, must be considered from a final or purposive point of view as well as from a causal view. The second is that symbols do not have a fixed meaning but must be understood within the metaphorical content of the dream. The last is concerned with the future orientation of the dream; thus, " . . . dreams have a prospective function . . . an anticipation of future conscious achievements, something like a preliminary exercise or sketch" . . . (11) All three of these issues will be further discussed below.

The writings of Adler himself are quite clear on certain aspects of dream theory, but vague and even contradictory on other aspects. This can be partly attributed to the fact that much of his writing was actually hastily composed from lectures and then inadequately translated. Later Adlerians have done a much more precise job of describing Adlerian dream theory and I will draw freely from them.

The Function of the Dream

1. The future orientation of the dream.

"Individual Psychology regards dreams as originating in unfinished and unsolved problems about which the individual is concerned and which he has been unable to solve during the day . . . such a conception implies that every dream in some way points to the future." (1, 74)

"A dream is a bridge that connects the problem which confronts the dreamer with his goal of attainment. In this way a dream will often come true because the dreamer will be training for his part during the dream and will be thus preparing for it to come true.[2] (2)

---

[2] This statement by Adler seems very close to the concept of wish-fulfillment, at least in a certain sense.

It is therefore one function of the dream to make plans for future behavior.

"The direction of the activity and therefore the anticipatory, prescient function of the dream is always clearly discernible; it foreshadows the preparations developed in connection with the actual difficulties encountered . . . " (3, 217)

2. The rehearsal function of the dream.

"Adler regards the immediate (as opposed to long term) problems as the pivot of the dream . . . it is a graphic rehearsal of the attitudes we shall adopt on waking" (14, 81).

"A dream is often a trial solution . . . " (15, 52).

Thus, one function of the dream is to rehearse for the future activity of the dreamer. Various coping methods are tried out for size and sometimes a choice is made, or at least a solution is discarded.

3. The self-deception purpose of the dream.

The dream uses metaphorical expressions. "The dream has a forward aim . . . it puts on an edge on the dreamer for the solution of a problem in his own particular way . . . it does this not on the basis of common sense . . . but metaphorically, in comparative pictures, somewhat in the manner of a poet when he wishes to arouse feelings and emotions"[3] (4, 259).

"The dreamer is engaged in molding attitude and dis position to coming events of life, storing up a certain reserve of feeling and emotion which could not be acquired in the daytime by contact with reality and logical thinking. He thus accumulates a certain irrational force to sustain him in the pursuit of his own goal . . . " (6, 163).

"It is the purpose of the dream to evoke feelings and emotions that lure the dreamer from the path of common sense" (13, 44).

---

[3] As Albee the dramatist and Dali the painter use "absurd" illogic to achieve an effect.

"The dream's most important purpose is to lead the dreamer away from common-sense . . . In the dream, therefore, the dreamer commits a self-deception" (4, 259).

In order to understand this concept of self-deception, it is important to understand what Adler meant by the term *common sense*. He does not use it to mean "horse sense" or practical wisdom but rather what Sullivan called consensual validation. The dreamer therefore uses a private language and private logic, valid only for himself and not subject to consensual validation.

The concept of self-deception is best explained by Dreikurs: "One cause for this apparent non-sense of the dream is . . . the lack of verbal logic. However . . . this is not the only reason why dreams remain obscure. Even the . . . psychotherapist, who (understands) the dreams of his patients, fails to grasp the meaning of his own dream. This reluctance to interpret correctly one's own dream is the consequence of the psychological function of the dream, namely to create certain emotions. All emotions serve the purpose of fortifying attitudes and actions. Their strength lies in the fact that their purpose is not recognized. If one realizes for what purpose one stimulates one's own emotions, . . . if one could admit that all these emotions are self-created for a very definite purpose . . . such admission would deprive the . . . emotion of its powerful drive. For this reason dreams must remain shrouded in mystery to be effective." (9)

4. The "factory of emotions"

The foregoing material has certainly suggested that the dream purposefully creates an emotional state in the dreamer. Individual Psychology has as an axiom that behavior is organized toward a final goal and that emotions are the *catalysts* of action. The emotions themselves serve as instruments to be used by the "actor" and are evoked by his cognitive tendencies, his thoughts and perceptions.[4]

---

[4] Thus, the depressed patient will keep himself sad and discouraged by constantly thinking morbid thoughts and finding fault with himself. Other schools of thought consider the depressive's self-blame to be self-punishment. The Adlerian claims that self-blame is necessary in order to stay depressed.

"Through the picture of the dream a certain emotion is created which then is carried into the new day, regardless of whether the dreamer remembers the dream or not. The dream can be called the "factory of emotions" (Alfred Adler), because that is the function of the dream . . . " (9)

"The purpose of the dreams must be in the feelings they arouse. The dream is only the means, the instrument, to stir up feelings. The goal of the dream is the feelings it leaves behind" (5, 98).

This concept is uniquely Adlerian and in my opinion represents the most important contribution that Individual Psychology has made to the understanding of the dream. Thus, according to this hypothesis, a nightmare occurs because the dreamer *has some private reason for frightening* himself and so on.

The following example was given me by Rudolf Dreikurs: A patient reported a dream in which he was in jail. He did not recall other dream elements. He did not understand the dream and could not offer associations except to say that he would not like being in jail. Dreikurs asked him if he had done something wrong or illegal or if he contemplated or had contemplated the same. The patient then confessed that he had compiled a fraudulent income tax return, but the next morning had thought better of it and redid the return to remove the fraudulent features and then posted the honest return with his check. He had made this decision the morning after the dream. However, he did not see the connection between the dream and his subsequent behavior until Dreikurs pointed it out to him.

The dream created a mood through a metaphor. It was the complete equivalent of a conscious decision to redo the tax return; but couched as a metaphor was much more evocative of emotions than would be rational thinking, which tends toward objectivity and dispassion.

It is *not* necessary for the dream to be consciously recalled for it to do its work of evoking a mood, any more than it is necessary to consciously recall a decision in order for that decision to influence subsequent behavior.

5. The preservation of sleep.

Adlerian writings have said nothing about Freud's statement that the dream serves to preserve sleep. I can vividly remember one morning dreaming that I was getting dressed and awakening to find that I was still in bed undressed. I freely admit that I wished to remain asleep rather than to get up and go to my early morning class. That dream certainly expressed a wish to remain asleep. However, this is not quite what Freud meant by the sleep preserving function of the dream.[5]

It is my impression that dreams occur during *light,* rather than heavy sleep. The physiologists will probably have the final word on this matter.

The Relationship Between Dream and Life Style

The Adlerian literature makes several statements concerning the relationship between dreams and the life style of the dreamer.

"In dreams we produce the pictures which will arouse the emotions we need for our purposes, that is, for solving problems confronting us at the time of the dream, in accordance with the particular style of life which is ours." (2)

" . . . they create a frame of mind in accordance with the style of life." . . . " the dream . . . selects from a thousand possible images only those that are favorable to its aims . . . in the interests of the style of life." (4, 260)

"The purpose of dreams is to support the style of life against the demands of common sense." (5, 100)

"The style of life is best shown by dreams which are often repeated . . . " (4, 263)

The above statements seem to add little to our understanding of the dream *per se.* All behavior, according to Individual Psychology, may reveal the basic personality tendencies which Adlerians call the *life style* and dreams need not be expected to reveal these more than other aspects

---

[5] Among some children, the fear of having "bad dreams" can lead to attempts to avoid sleep. At one time in my own childhood I tried to avoid bad dreams by saying a little prayer before I went to sleep. I am happy to report that my method worked and I shall be glad to teach it to anyone who is interested.

of behavior or other mental processes. Furthermore, the life style is a unifying pattern, a personal construct, which governs the direction of behavior and thus produces a selective movement in line with itself, like Sullivan's *self-system,* Allport's *proprium,* Horney's *idealized image* and Berne's *script.*

Modern Adlerians are much more likely to stress the immediate future for which the dreamer prepares himself and an analysis of dreams does not lead to an understanding of the life style as does an analysis of the family constellation or of the earliest childhood recollections, two unique diagnostic instruments devised by Adler.

Furthermore, recurrent dreams sometimes are best understood as an attempt to cope with recent traumas (as noted by Freud) and do not necessarily reveal basic tendencies.

However, "The style of life is the master of dreams. It (the dream) will always arouse the feelings we need. We would approach the problems in the same way whether we dreamed or not; but the dream offers a support and justification for the (goals chosen) in the style of life." (5, 101)

Thus, the dream, like any other phenomenal event, can be pressed into the service of the individual's movement toward his intended goal, reinforcing his underlying attitudes and providing emotional support for his decisions.

The Language of the Dream

Adlerians follow Freud in considering that the dream uses mechanisms that are not compatible with most of the realities of every day life.

"For the solution of an undecided question . . . abstract and infantile comparisons are at hand, . . . frequently suggesting more expressive and more poetical images. For example, an impending decision may be replaced (symbolized) by a school examination, a strong opponent by an older brother, the idea of victory by a flight to the sky, and a danger by an abyss or fall." (3, 222)

Way compares the dream to a work of art which expresses a whole chain of ideas through a few details. Each dream is a totality, a crystalization into an image and a mood.

"Each detail of the dream is symbolic of the whole inter-related background . . . The dream is composed with frag-ments of things seen, conversations heard, emotions and sensations already experienced, all the scraps and rem-nants of perception worked into a kind of 'collage' . . .[6] As Freud pointed out, the dream has no pictorial way of render-ing logical connections expressed in speech by such words as *and, but, either-or, though, because.*" (14,84)

"Both poem and dream depend for their effect on tech-nique." (14, 86) Each detail, says Way, is reckoned as part of the whole structure. Thus, a contradictory dream points to a contradiction in the thoughts or attitudes of the dreamer. A nonsense dream is a way of saying, "This is just a lot of nonsense."

The dream makes extensive use of symbolic imagery. We used to consider that dreaming was merely thinking of a kind that went on while the conscious faculties were inhibited but recent dream deprivation studies indicate that dreaming may be something more, something necessary to the well-being of the organism in some manner we do not yet understand. According to Individual Psychology, symbols are contingent upon culture and change with culture (which also contradicts the idea that dreams necessarily reveal the life style). While Freud considered many symbols universal, the Adlerian is more likely to feel that the issues which appear in dreams may be universal (cf. Jung's archetypes) but the symbols are seldom so. (12) There are exceptions to every rule. An example is the tendency of the hungry person to dream of food (an example of a wish fulfillment dream).

There are however common symbols which appear in dreams. Thus wild animals usually refer to the dangers of life, clothes and hair to the self-image of the dreamer, face-less people to the person not known or not understood, trav-eling dreams to movement through life, crossing a river to making a decision, nudity to a fear of exposure, small animals

---

[6] Freud's statement that the manifest content of the dream often contains the previous day's residue.

to children or younger siblings, ice cream to luxuries or "goodies," being chased to feeling pressed, being heavy-legged and unable to run to feeling inadequate to a task, etc.

Many dreams can be classified into various types. Thus nightmares are a dreamer's way of frightening himself about some matter. Triumph dreams (as in a sexual triumph) indicate that the dreamer feels he is accomplishing something. Dreams about recently deceased relatives indicate that the dreamer has not yet buried his dead. There are probably exceptions to all these rules.

In general, the more vivid the dream, the more the dreamer is trying to impress himself (or his therapist). Some dreams come in three acts, perhaps with different symbols recapitulating the same themes, and all the acts of the dream must be placed in apposition in order to understand the message of the dream.

Dream fragments can best be understood as cross-sections through the dream. A number of fragments can constitute a sketch of the whole dream.

The role of the dreamer, whether he is main actor, peripheral observer, victim, hero, etc. is important in understanding the dream.

When a dreamer "knows" that he is dreaming it is an indication that he is not willing to let himself go in his private logic completely. Sometimes a dreamer will wake himself up if he doesn't like the way his dream is going. (cf. Freud's censor).

Because the Adlerian therapist asks for and interprets dreams, the dreams of people in therapy take on added significance because they become part of the dialogue between patient and therapist, and often have a direct reference to the therapy itself. The first dream, shortly before or after the first interview seems always to refer to the therapy. A sudden appearance of dreams in a non-dreamer usually points to increased willingness to reveal oneself (to himself as well as to the therapist). The cessation of dreams means that the patient has become unwilling to reveal himself further or that he is finished dealing with the problem area concerned with his previous series of dreams. A dream of change may anticipate therapeutic change, a dream of childhood may signify that the dreamer will move backward. Incessant dreams are sometimes used as a form of resistance to therapy, the patient filling up the therapeutic hour with reports of his dreams and leaving the therapist in the dark about the every day life of the patient.

Relapses can be signaled in dreams: A patient dreamt that he fell off a cliff and drifted slowly to the bottom without hurting himself. He then got to his feet and walked through a door in the side of the cliff. The door closed after him and the dream ended. A week later he became psychotic.

When Do We Dream?

Adler seemed to be of the opinion that the dream is purposefully used to circumvent reality and the rational processes:

"We dream only if we are not sure of the solution of our problems, only if reality is pressing in on us even in our sleep and offering us difficulties. This is the task of the dream: to meet the difficulties . . . and to provide a solution." (5, 99)

". . . if an individual is confronted by a problem which he doesn't wish to solve along the lines of common sense, he can confirm his attitudes by the feelings which are aroused in his dreams." (5, 100)

The dream . . . "in itself a sign that the dreamer feels inadequate to solve the problems by common sense alone." (2)

Adler even suggests that the absence of dreams indicates an "adjusted" (conflict-free) person. "The more the individual goal agrees with reality, the less a person dreams. Very courageous people dream rarely, for they deal adequately with (problems) in the day time." (2)

And again, "Dreaming is the adversary of common sense . . . people who do not like to be deluded by their feelings, who prefer to proceed in a (rational) way, do not dream often . . . " (5, 101)

Finally, " . . . a metaphorical conception of one's situation is a way of escape from it" (as in the dream). (6, 163)

The above suggests that the non-dreamer is somehow more realistic than the dreamer and that the latter somehow lacks "courage." These ideas will be examined later in the critique.

The Clinical Use of the Dream

While Adler and other Adlerian writers made many general remarks about dreams and gave numerous examples with interpretation, the writings themselves seem more concerned with the therapist's use of the dream in order to understand the patient. Little has been written to show how the Adlerian therapist actually uses the dream in his relationship with the patient. Exceptions are found in Wexberg: "The task of the psychotherapist will be to interpret (dreams) . . . into the scheme of this personality and so step by step to complete the portrait of the patient's character (in line with the life style)."

"The communication of dreams must in general be expressly demanded of the patient . . . For the purpose of therapy dream interpretation offers advantages of two kinds: First the patient learns, through the successful and convincing interpretation of his dreams, that there really are mental processes which (seem) to be withdrawn from his willing and thinking . . . which . . . on closer consideration reveal themselves as valid portions of his responsible actively thinking and acting personality . . . Secondly, the *denouement* of the dream shows . . . with great clearness in what sense the patient is inclined to solve his actual problems."

"In the interpretation of all dreams . . . one must never go further than is compatible with the state of the patient's knowledge (ability to understand dynamics) at the time . . . in a few weeks . . . in the interpretation of his ideas and dreams, the patient shall be able almost to dispense with the physician's help." (16, 143-147)

"The analysis of dreams," says Dreikurs, "is indispensable in modern psychotherapy . . . The need to use dreams . . . emanates from their usefulness to indicate problems which otherwise might not come to the surface . . . (also . . . Dreams provide the most dramatic experience for patient and therapist alike when they reveal the changes which occur in the patient during therapy. One patient had . . . (all short) dreams and without any action. He did in his dreams what he did in life; he . . . figured *out* the best way of a problem. When his dreams started to move and become active, he started to move in his life, too." (9)

Walter Bonime's book, *The Clinical Use of Dreams* (7) is perhaps the most useful volume on dreams that has been published in many decades. As I read the book from the Adlerian point of view I was both pleased and surprised that I could find nothing with which an Adlerian could disagree. Indeed, I wish I had written the book. Ullman's foreword to the book pointed out the similarity of ideas in Adler and Bonime and some of Bonime's formulations found a startling reverberation in me. For example, Bonime has divided the elements of the dream into 1) action, 2) individual, 3) surroundings and (4 feelings. I had for myself formulated the elements of the dream from the point of view of a dramatic creation. The particular four elements I had used were 1) the narrative, 2) the cast, 3) the setting and 4) the mood. Throughout the book one can find statements that fit the view points of Adlerians. I certainly do not wish to detract from Dr. Bonime's accomplishment, nor do I claim primacy for the Adlerians. I suspect, however, that his book is becoming a text in our training centers.

The Adlerian therapist, thus, asks for dreams from the patient, uses them to understand and define problem areas, to predict the near future direction of movement of the patient, to fill out his understanding of the patient's characteristic lines of movement (the life style), to alert himself to the patient's movement in the therapeutic relationship, to show the patient these aspects of himself, and to teach the patient to observe and understand his own dynamics.

My colleagues and I have also encouraged dreaming when therapy has bogged down in stalemate or has run out of fresh material. We then suggest to the patient that he recall his dreams. If he says he cannot we ask him to follow our instructions; which are, for three weeks to keep paper and pencil by his bedside and upon awakening to write down any fragments he can recall before he even thinks about anythinge else. If the patient is cooperative, he can always report dreams by the end of three weeks. When we consider a patient "closed-up" and unable to reveal himself either to himself or the therapist, we will also encourage dreaming for the purpose of promoting a more introspective and self-examining attitude. The successful interpretation of a dream may be a means of "getting through" to the patient where other methods have failed. Indeed, the patient may be willing to reveal more intimacies in his dreams than in a face to face confrontation with the therapist; the reporting of a dream is usually less threatening than a direct admission.

One patient dreamed that he was a dinner guest of a couple. While the host sat eating at the head of the table, the dreamer surreptitiously fondled the hostess who responded, warmly. In the dream he felt ashamed of deceiving his host while a guest at his table. In association, he then offered a fact about his sex life which had previously been ashamed to admit to me; namely, that he was having a sexual affair with his landlady while having a friendship with her husband.

Patients' dreams also provide grist for the mill in group therapy. One group technique can be called, "You tell me your dream and I'll tell you mine." As implied by the name, the telling and interpreting of dreams becomes a part of the group activity. Another useful technique is the psycho-dramatic re-enactment of the dream in the group session. I learned a special variation of this from a patient of Dr. Fritz Perls, the Gestalt therapist. The patient acts out every role in his dream; thus, if he dreams of a car he acts out the role of "car" and associates to the role he is acting.

One of my colleagues, R. Postel, uses dreams in a particular way with sociopathic patients. He instructs the patient that they will discuss only his dreams and nothing else during the therapy session. If the patient has no dreams, there will be no session. He claims that this promotes a quicker and better rapport with this kind of patient than do the more usual techniques.

One other point needs mention. Patients may offer dreams and it is doubtful that detailed association is required or desirable in all cases. Furthermore, some dream meanings are very easily made evident. In these cases, the therapist may content himself with only interpreting the "headlines" of the dream (1, 79). On the other hand, a patient can use dreams defensively. As previously mentioned, incessant reporting of dreams may lead the therapist away from important therapeutic issues. A patient once became annoyed with what he called my "hot-shot" interpretations and brought several long complicated dreams, saying, "o.k., let's see how good a job you can do with *these* dreams." I guessed his intention and confronted him with it, and received a big recognition smile in return. Another patient would bring up dreams in order to change the subject whenever the discussion became uncomfortable for her. At these times I would refuse to be sidetracked into an examination of the dream.

Generally, Adlerians decline to interpret isolated dreams when they do not know the dreamer or his life situation. The interpretation of dreams as a parlor exercise has thus never found favor among them.

A Critique of Some Adlerian Statements About the Dream

This paper has reviewed the Adlerian literature[7] as well as adding some ideas of myself and my colleagues. The most recent reference in this review is to a book written in 1950. It is thus 17 years since Adlerians have written seriously about dreams and many of the statements are already half a century old and may display aged psychological language or even careless statements. For example:

"Those with a good adoption to life dream rarely . . . since they solve their problems adequately during the day."[8] (14,77) Modern Adlerians cannot accept this statement. It is not supported conceptually by Adlerian theory or by empirical evidence. Today, we should be inclined to agree with Fromm who considers dreaming as part of the "forgotten

---

[7] The only major Adlerian work on the dream not reviewed in this paper is also the only full length book on the subject by Brachfeld, F. O. *Come Interpretare i Sogni*, Milan, Garzanti, 1951. It is available in Spanish, but not in English. Unfortunately, my Italian is limited, but I have been told that this work summarizes the usual Adlerian ideas.

[8] Way, the author of this statement, points out that F. Plewa, another Adlerian, disagrees with it.

language" in a rationalistic and mechanistic age. (10) It is probable that this idea grew out of the fact that vivid dreams are often found in the anxious and troubled person. We are now of the opinion that any person who has an active fantasy life may recall dreams frequently and freely and that all people dream every night, whether they remember or not.

"As a rule, people who are courageous seldom dream because they use the daytime for working out their problems, but in everyone's life situations may arise which for a time remain insoluble and as a consequence give rise to the formation of dream." (1, 77)

Today, we would agree that conflict situations probably increase dreaming; because, after all, it is one function of the dream to solve problems, or at least to rehearse possible solutions. However, to say that courageous people dream less is to make an unfounded statement. Even worse, we recognize that the individual who reports, "I never dream," is often complacent and full of blind spots, exerting rigid control over his thoughts and feelings. Therefore, we would be in danger of confounding courage with smugness and rigidity. REM studies, of course have rather firmly established that everyone dreams and apparently that dreaming is a normal and necessary function.

Adler says, "the unintelligibility of the dream is not a matter of choice, but a necessity." (4, 261) The purpose of the dream are achieved not by "reason and judgement," but by "emotion and mood" (2). "A metaphorical conception of one's situation is a way of escape from it." (6, 163)

Actually, not all dreams are unintelligible. Some are quite easily understood. Furthermore, the juxtaposition of "reasons and judgement" versus "emotion and mood" smacks too much of the Appolonian *versus* Dionysian and implies that emotions exclude reason or disagree with it. It is rather that the dream achieves an effect like the dramatist or the artist does. The message sent by the dream may be quite subject to consensual validation and all of the metaphors and artistic techniques may be quite recognizable to the dreamer. The dream is also a legitimate way of experiencing life.

Also, if one really wants to deceive oneself, one can use rational thinking just as effectively as dreaming. It seems, therefore, more appropriate to say that *some* dreams perform their intended function better if they are unintelligible to the dreamer (as when a person does not wish to admit his real motives to himself). There is no reason to elevate rational conscious thinking to such a high plane at the expense of metaphorical thinking.

Adler is reported to have said that he stopped dreaming[9] because he became so well able to interpret his dreams that they could not perform their function any longer (13, 45). Perhaps Adler was convinced that it was the purpose of the dream to deceive and therefore chose to avoid recalling any more dreams.

Wexberg states, " . . . the dream is a form of preparation for the future. Dreams are . . . better adapted than working thoughts to the task of preparing emotional attitudes." (15, 54) This statement ignores what every therapist knows; that selective perception, selective memory, rationalization, neurotic symptoms and many other mental operations are well adapted to evoking emotional attitudes. Dreams have no monopoly on preparing a person for choosing a course of action in life.

"Short dream," says Adler, "indicate that the present problems are such that the dreamer desires to find a 'short cut.'" (6, 164) In a later publication he says, (Short dreams) show that a question has answered concisely and decided upon quickly." (4, 263).

The second statement seems logical, the first seems to be rather extravagant. It may be true of *some* short dreams (see the above example by Dreikurs) but it is hardly likely to be true of all of them.

---

[9] One should say he stopped *recalling* his dreams. In defense of Adler I can recall a repetitive dream of my own which stopped completely when I understood its functions. I used to dream from time to time that one of my parents was sick or dead. I would awake worried and call or write immediately (they lived in another city). I eventually realized that the dream occurred only when I had neglected to call or write them for several weeks and that the purpose of the dream was to induce me to do my filial duty. With this realization the dreams ended. (My psychoanalytic colleagues may say the dream showed a death wish, but without denying that I found my filial duties onerous I prefer my own interpretation. It was the obligation I wanted to kill, not the person).

Some Additional Formulations

Adlerian theory discusses the dream from the point of view of its expressive nature, its purposive nature and its representational nature (or symbolology). Not enough attention has been paid in the literature to the therapeutic uses of the dream. The functions of the dream have been described as rehearsing solutions for solving problems, creating an emotional climate which will lead to the course of action chosen (consciously or otherwise) by the dreamer and operating to overcome conscious hesitation or reluctance to move in the chosen direction. Sometimes, one can discern in the dreams elements of the dreamer's style of life. Some dreams are for wish-fulfillment, some are perhaps intended to preserve sleep. The dream is usually much more concerned with the immediate future, but some dreams point to long term trends (this is especially true of childhood dreams which are recalled in adult life). The great majority of dreams can be seen as containing a message to the self. In dreams during therapy, the patient may be more interested in sending a message to the therapist.

No doubt some dreams can speak to both patient and therapist at the same time. When I was in the army a bedraggled basic trainee was sent to me because of neurasthenic complaints and an inability to fit into his platoon. He was a college graduate from New York City and felt intellectually quite superior to his platoon mates who were country boys from the Carolinas. His attitude toward them was timid and sneering and he had not endeared himself to them. I made some interpretations to him in the first interview to which he responded with surprise that I was so sure I knew him so well. He brought a dream to the second interview.

He was watching a large cylindrical object mounted on a flat carriage and rolling down Fifth Avenue in Manhattan. At intervals one edge of the cylinder would arise and point skyward, then it would descent and lie level again. Some kind of hydraulic machinery was involved. He was impressed at first, then decided it was nothing special.

He then admitted that he had also been impressed by some of my interpretations of the first interview. I established that he mistakenly assumed I came from New York (since he considered me intelligent he jumped to the conclusion that I must be a New Yorker).

I did not quite know how to take the dream. He did not make any associations but I made some of my own. The dream seemed partly complimentary to me and partly antagonistic. I felt that I was being called, "a big prick on wheels from New York who wasn't anything special after all" and my subsequent relationship with this patient bore out that it was his intention to show that he was intellectually superior to me just as he was to all the other soldiers in the training camp.

Adlerians have neglected two items which I myself feel are proper functions of dreams. One is that the dream which is a message to the self is often a *self-clarification* for the dreamer, used by him to clarify for himself his own inner feelings so that he can decide where he stands.

One young man was on the verge of falling in love with a girl when she suddenly began to prefer the company of another man. The young man's past tendency in such situations had been to make a graceful exit from the scene. He was in doubt about the depth of his own feeling for the girl and his pride was hurt. He dreamed that he was in the courtroom where the girl was on trial for witchcraft and that he was acting as prosecutor and angrily accusing her. In the dream he grew more angry and struck her. At this point he awoke. He reviewed the dream for himself and decided that his feeling of affection for her must be genuine or he would not have been so angry, nor would he have seen her as a witch. He then decided to pursue his relationship with her and eventually persuaded her to marry him.

The second item is that the dream falls into a class of mental phenomena which include fantasy and reverie. It is my opinion that some night dreams have the same purpose as some daydreams; namely, to provide some entertainment for oneself, and I suspect that dreams are not as involuntary as Dr. Ullman seems to say. I can recall, as a small child, how curious and fascinating I found my own dreams and how I looked forward to having them. Dreaming seemed so much more pleasant than spending the whole night doing nothing.

REM Studies and Adlerian Theory

There is no doubt that all psychological theories of dreaming must now take into account the findings of the REM researchers. Dreaming now seems to have a physiologic function and dream deprivation to produce specific and recognizable effects. Early assumptions that the hallucination was the equivalent of a waking dream have received some support. The non-recall of dreams can now be approached with more confidence by the psychologists as *their* problem, since REM studies seem to establish that all men ordinarily dream. Adlerians would suspect that dreaming has a necessary psychological function rather simply a physiological one, or being merely a by-product of some rhythmic biological process. All human activity, for Adlerians, is arranged according to an overall organismic system principle which they call the Life Style. All recurring phenomena, such as dreaming, memory, perception, etc., are integrated into the overall system.

Dreams may have an excretory function, but as Dr. Bonime says, dreams show selectivity — are themselves *creations,* are messages. From the psychological point of view, the excretory function seems less important, the other functions become crucial and *determining,* especially determining the intensity, mood, theme, symbols and recollection of the dream. As Dr. Whitman and his collaborators point out, the psychology of dreams must not be confused with the biology of dreaming. (17)

One new area of dream theory must be explored: the instinctive nature of the dream. Dr. Whitman and his collaborators have already pointed out that the REM studies evoke anew the whole question of instinctive processes in man. (17) It is certainly true that the newer developments in psychoanalysis have tended to neglect instinct theory and that neo-Freudian theories have, like Adler, focused on interpersonal processes. No doubt the Adlerians deserve a little credit for making Freudian instinct theory unpopular. However, Adlerians have never denied the existence of instincts or their basic importance. They have objected to psychoanalytic instinct theories which neglected social aspects of man's nature and his own creative power to order and modify his instincts and objected strenuously to the use of pschoanalytic instinct theory to explain the functional psychiatric disorders. It is the overall Adlerian *view of man* that is so different from the orthodox psychoanalytic view.

Nevertheless, the newly discovered physiologic aspects of dreaming, its rhythmic nature, the consequences of disruption of the dreaming all point to a coming revival in the study of man's instincts. Adlerians will watch this development with great interest. We have our own instinct theory although we don't call it that. The life style, the law of compensation, *gemeinschaftsgefühl* and many other concepts are part of that theory of instincts. However, I expect that the newer developments will follow the lead of the European ethologists rather than the psychoanalysts. In some ways, what we already know of dreaming fits in with the theories of Lorenz and Tinbergen. Terms such as taxis, innate releasing mechanism, sign stimulus and vacuum discharge may soon become common parlance in our discussions of dreams.

REFERENCES

1. Adler, Alexandra. *Guiding Human Misfits.* London: Faber and Faber, 1948.

2. Adler, Alfred. On the interpretation of dreams. Int. J. Indiv. Psychol. 2, 1: 3-16, 1936.

3. —— *The Practice and Theory of Individual Psychology.* Totowa, N.J.: Littlefield, Adams, 1959.

4. —— *Social Interest: A Challenge to Mankind. New York:* Putnam & Sons, 1964.

5. —— *What Life Should Mean To You.* New York: Putnam & Sons, 1958.

6. —— *Problems of Neurosis.* New York: Harper Torchbooks, 1967.

7. Bonime, Walter. *The Clinical Use of Dreams.* New York: Basic Books, 1962.

8. Brachfeld, F. O. *Come Interpretare i. Sogni.* Milan. Garzanti, 1951.

9. Dreikurs, Rudolf. The meaning of dreams. Chicago Med. Sch. Quart. 5:3, 1944.

10. Fromm, Erich. *The Forgotten Language.* New York: Grove Press, 1957.

11. Jung, Carl G. General aspects of dream psychology. in Jung, C.G. *Collected Works,* 8 pp. 237-280. London: Routledge and Kegan Paul, 1960.

12. Mosak, Harold H. & Todd F. J. Selective Perception in the interpretation of symbols. J. Abnorm. and soc. Psychol., 1952, 4, 255-256.

13. Orgler, Hertha. *Alfred Adler: The Man and His Work.* New York: Liveright, 1963.

14. Way, Lewis. *Adler's Place in Psychology.* London: Allen and Unwin, 1950.

15. Wexberg, Erwin. *Individual Psychology.* New York: Cosmopolitan, 1929.

16. —— *Individual Psychological Treatment.* Chicago: Alfred Adler Institute, 1970.

17. Whitman, R. M., Kramer, M., Ornstein, P. H., Baldridge, B. J. The physiology, psychology and utilization of dreams. Amer. J. Psychiat. 124: 3, 287-302, Sept. 1967.

THE USES AND ABUSES OF SEX *

Introduction

So large a subject as sex is a daring one for the author of a small paper such as this. The reader will inevitably find large aspects of the subject omitted or shabbily treated in such a brief purview. Let me then make clear that this paper concerns itself with a limited topic: a particular way of assessing sexual behavior.

Other systems of thought approach the topic of sex according to the intentions and viewpoints of the particular systems. It would seem appropriate to mention some of these systems briefly and then specify the system herein used.

Ways of Looking at Sex

Best known to scientists is the biological way of viewing sex. The purpose of sex is reproduction of the species, and sexual behavior is mainly the method of accomplishment. The organism is considered to have sexual drives that are expressed in courtship behavior (including aggressiveness), territorial behavior, nesting behavior, and other behavior that brings the male and female together and provides some protection for the young. The sex drives sometimes lead to conflict among those animals that, like man, live in social communities.

Among psychologists, the psychoanalytic system is probably the best known (though not necessarily accepted) way of looking at sex. According to this system, the sex drives are physiologically based, located in the id, repressed, when unacceptable, by the ego and superego. Oedipal wishes are universal and the sex drives are to a great extent in conflict with civilized society, which abhoring incest, acts as a

---

* Reprinted from Journal of Religion and Health, Vol. 6, No. 4, October 1967

repressive force. Much of a human being's life is therefore a search for pleasure. Sublimation of sex drives is necessary and desirable in order to permit man to live in society.

A third systematic way of viewing sex is found in the Judeo-Christian religious tradition of the Western world. Judaism and Christianity both define proper and improper sexual behavior. Sex is both sacrament and sin. Sexual drives are temptations of the flesh and require bridling, except in "proper" circumstances. The more repressive religious views suspect all sexual pleasure of being sinful.

The Counselor's Dilemma

Secular counselors for many years have tried to use a nonmoralistic way of looking at sexual behavior. To a great extent, these counselors felt obliged to correct some of the repressive and punitive excesses of a puritanical tradition. It seemed useful to inform patients that masturbation did not turn a person into a monster, that occasional forbidden sexual thought did not indicate insanity, that many sexual desires were normal and appropriate, that women were entitled to sexual satisfaction, etc. These same counselors were well aware of the dangers of certain kinds of sexual behavior and did not condone excessive, socially disruptive, or ethically distasteful behavior.

There is far less guilt today about sexual behavior; indeed, there is often so little guilt as to alarm both clergy and secular counselor. Today's patient is as apt to suffer from sexual ennui as from unsatisfied prurience. Freer sexual behavior does not seem to have reduced the hard job of achieving meaningful and satisfying sexual activity.

The pastoral counselor has always been in a dilemma. Sometimes, in order to "accept" the patient, he must be silent concerning behavior he considers sinful. If he threatens the patient with the nether regions, he feels that he is perhaps neglecting to understand, to interpret properly, to uncover dynamics, and so forth. His life was simpler when the psychodynamics of behavior could be simply traced back to the machinations of the adversary. It's always nice to recognize the enemy, because it makes the choice of behavior easier.

Another View of Sex

It is possible to view sex from another angle: *for what is the sexual behavior used?* Such a point of view partakes of the transactional, the teleological, and the ethical. It is a view that can be used in straightforward, moral (yet not moralistic) discussion. The criterion by which the act is judged becomes the social purpose for which it is used. Social purposes are not hard to judge. Behavior is either socially useful or socially useless. Destructive sexual behavior would always seem to be useless. So, it would seem, is unethical sexual behavior. The existence of sexual drives is taken for granted. Also taken for granted is the idea that sexual behavior is under the individual's control (much more than psychoanalytic theory has been willing to admit). The drive to defecate is more immediate and I suspect more intense than the sex drive, but most of us seem to make it to the proper receptacle most of the time.

Sex is therefore something a person does, not just something that happens to him. Why a person uses sex in one way rather than another will be related to his own personal opinion of sex and of life. For example, if he sees life as a competitive striving to get, to have, to achieve, then his sexual behavior will reflect these same propensities and he will have trained himself over the years to use sex for personal triumph in a competitive arena. Sufficient unto each individual case will be the analysis of the reasons for one or another particular use or abuse of sex, and to this analysis the counselor can betake himself.

When is sex useful? When it promotes what we ordinarily consider "good": social harmony, pleasure, love, and so forth. When is it useless? When it is destructive, socially isolating, produces suffering, etc.

Before we turn our attention to the uses and abuses of sex, let me caution the reader that I will not speak specifically of marriage. Like it or not, much sexual behavior (e.g., masturbation) takes place outside marriage. For the purpose of this discussion, it will sometimes be appropriate to consider the behavior in a marital situation and sometimes not.

Furthermore, I shall not pay any particular attention to the sexual perversions. By and large, they are all useless forms of sexual behavior from a social point of view, but their dynamics have been discussed in many other places and are not appropriate to the small task I have set myself in this paper.

The Uses of Sex

My colleague, Harold H. Mosak, and I have been teaching for a number of years[1] that there are at least six socially useful ways of using sex. The number is not magic; it was simply all we could think of at the time.

1. The first of these uses is reproduction. I suppose we list it first because it seems simpler to start with biology than anything else or because it makes us feel scientific. Reproduction, however, has psychological as well as biological meaning. One reason people sleep with each other is that they *want* to have children.

2. The second use of sex is for pleasure. It is not illegitimate for people to want to enjoy themselves, and sex is certainly a time-honored way.

3. A third use is to bring about a feeling of belonging. The sexual relationship can offer companionship, affection, and emotional closeness; it can produce a deep bond between the participating individuals, can promote love and end arguments. Such a use of sex almost *demands* those sentiments we name *love*. To know such a relationship means that one has been touched with a new understanding of life that never quite leaves one thereafter.

4. Sex, furthermore, requires co-operative endeavor and is therefore a kind of sharing that is more than a feeling of belonging. It is the kind of sharing that is missing when co-operation is missing, such as when a husband chafes impatiently in bed while his wife leisurely creams her face and puts up her hair in curlers. Conversely, it is also missing when the husband ejaculates prematurely and leaves his wife "high and dry." What is shared here is a mutual task. The amount

---

[1] At the Alfred Adler Institute in Chicago.

of co-operation required in sex is probably greater than that required in most other human relationships. Indeed, in my opinion, the ability of husband and wife to co-operate in bed is a mirror of their ability to co-operate in other aspects of their relationship.

Admittedly, sharing an experience adds to its pleasure, but pleasure has already been mentioned above.

5. Another legitimate use of sex is for the purpose of consolation. It is not generally recognized that sexual appetite often increases after the death of a loved one or another loss. An ancient story from Apuleus illustrates this. A wife was mourning her just-deceased husband in his tomb while nearby a soldier was guarding the bodies of some criminals who had been crucified. The soldier, hearing her weeping, entered the tomb to console her and remained. Meanwhile, the relatives of a criminal stole his body from the cross to bury it. In order to protect her new lover, the wife arranged for him to place her late husband's body on the empty cross. The story was probably told as a humorous example of the duplicity of women, but it also illustrates the use of sex as consolation. When one has been hurt or humiliated, has heard bad news, or feels sad for any reason, sex can console.

6. The sixth use of sex is for the purpose of self-affirmation. One can use sexual behavior to say that one is a man (or woman), that one is a lover, that something has been achieved, that one is worth while and acceptable, and that one is loved.

7. A lovely lady, a patient, once taught me how limited my own views were. In discussing sex with me, she described to me seven additional uses for sex that I have not previously considered. "Sometimes," she said, "you use sex just to encourage somebody."

"When you want to get the other person to do something?" I asked.

"Yes, that too, but also when you want to let him know you're on his side." We agreed to call this sex for the purpose of encouragement.

"Sometimes you go to bed with someone just for excitement."

"Well," I answered, "that's really a variety of pleasure."

"No, it's more than pleasure. It's when you want to stir things up, like getting him upset, or his wife upset, or getting your husband upset."

"I can't consider that a legitimate use of sex," I retorted with a straight face.

8. "How about sex for relaxation? It's better than sleeping pills."

"I'll accept that one," I answered.

9. Then she offered: "How about sex for distraction?"

"Of course," I said. "That reminds me of the lady with rheumatoid arthritis who never felt any pain when she was flat on her back with a man."

10. Warming to the subject, she continued, "The next thing is closeness."

"Do you mean sharing an experience or a feeling of belonging?"

"No. You can share an experience without getting close; but this is when you want the experience of being physically and emotionally close to somebody, like getting inside of someone's skin."

"I suspect," I answered, "that I would classify that under the *feeling of belonging,* but at this point I am willing to defer to your more experienced judgment. What else?"

11. "Sex," she said, "can be used as stimulation. If you're feeling lazy and don't feel like doing anything and can't get started, it's a good way to start the day off."

"I see," I mused. "Like a sitting-up exercise."

12. "Sex can also be a gift. It's something you give to somebody you like."

13. "And one more," she continued. "Sex is also used for getting acquainted."

"What do you mean?" I asked.

"It's a good way of getting to know somebody."

I will make no comment about the last mentioned use of sex; I will simply leave it to the reader to decide if he wants to include it among the list of legitimate uses.

The Abuses of Sex

It has perhaps already become obvious that sex is a common form of human behavior that can be used for a number of different purposes having little to do with its supposed biological function. This principle applies to other forms of behavior; e.g., eating. We eat to be sociable, for consolation, to pass the time, to explore new restaurants, and for other reasons little connected with hunger.

Sexual deviations, or perversions, are not my important topic. It is perhaps the purpose of many sexual symptoms to interfere with ordinary useful sexual behavior, but the abuses of sex will be discussed from a different point of view, among which can be classified the sexual deviations, such as homosexuality, and the sexual symptoms, such as premature ejaculation.

1. *Sex for mischief.* Apropos of my patient's suggestion that sex can be used to create excitement, a socially useless or destructive use of sex is for the purpose of making mischief. Mischievousness is a common form of behavior. One can use it to express rebellion against rules, to thumb one's nose at authority, to flout independence and willfulness, to have one's own way in spite of everything, and so on. Thus, a woman can flirt with all the men at a party (to the embarrassment of her escort), a girl can fall in love with a married man, a bored man can seek women for excitement, etc.

2. *Sex for distance.* The sexual sentiments are normally conjunctive, but what of those people who fear intimacy and wish to maintain distance between themselves and others? Certain sexual deviations are here put to good use. The exhibitionist has his sex at a distance from the other participant in his game. The fetishist substitutes a part for the person and in effect says, "This lovely part of you or article of your clothing is much more appealing than you are." Furthermore, the partner, even in apparently normal intercourse, is sometimes *object* rather than *person,* a pair of breasts and a

vagina rather than a living, breathing human being with interests and feelings of her own.

3. *Sex for domination.* In the thirties, Maslow did a series of studies on monkeys that showed that the dominant monkey in the group (male or female) asserted his dominance by performing copulating movements with any other monkey (of any sex), while his subjects demonstrated their submissiveness by presenting themselves in the proper position to be penetrated. Since there is often no real possibility for sexual gratification (as when a female dominates a male), it simply seems to be a way of establishing who is boss.

To some men, seducing a girl means putting something over on her. A woman may also try to dominate her husband by using sex as reward and withholding it as punishment in order to induce him to behave according to her wishes.

The medieval custom of *jus prima nocte* is, whatever else it may have been, also an example of the use of sex for the purpose of asserting dominance.

4. *Sex for suffering.* For any number of psychological reasons, some people want to create a situation in which they can claim to be suffering. Sex, like other aspects of behavior, can be used for this purpose. For example, one can suffer because one is "sexually frustrated," a rather arbitrary state of mind that permits the so-called frustrated person to feel sorry for himself. A girl can indulge herself sexually with the wrong person, with predictable consequences, and then feel that her life has been ruined. She may even try to make a career out of her one mistake in order to achieve a life of glorious tragedy. A more common example of sex as suffering can be seen in those women who submit to their husbands in a martyred way (because men are supposed to have "animal needs" and require sexual service from their wives), enjoying their own "long-suffering goodness" and feeling no sexual pleasure while their husbands cavort.

5. *Sex to demonstrate success or failure.* Sex is frequently an arena for competitive combat. For many men, virility means success, impotence or premature ejaculation means failure. One patient (who felt like a failure in most areas of

life) used the following idea to convince himself that he was a failure: During intercourse, he would imagine masochistic scenes in order to heighten his pleasure. He then concluded that he was sexually a failure because he indulged himself in masochistic fantasies. Among adolescent boys, sexual activity is used for boasting in order to impress one's peers. The seduction of others (both hetero- and homosexual) is often used as a measure of success, a victory that enhances one.

A common example is also the idealization of orgasm as a measure of success or failure. A woman may feel like a failure because she infrequently reaches a climax or her husband may feel that *he* is a failure because he was not able to induce her to reach climax.

6. *Sex for vanity.* Closely allied to the use of sex for success and failure is its use in the service of one's own vanity. "Look how great I am," "Look how well I do it," "Look how many people I can make fall in love with me," or "I am so irresistible that men can't help looking at me every time I walk into a room" are examples of the prideful thoughts that underlie such behavior. One patient looked forward to marriage because she was intrigued by the idea that she was sexually desirable. She was less interested in intercourse than in the game of keeping her husband attracted to her. After the honeymoon she made a habit of parading naked in front of her husband and was quite upset when he didn't get aroused. She came to me with the complaint, "I think there's something wrong with my husband. He's not sexually attracted to me." The husband defended himself, saying, "She expects an erection all day long just because she's walking up and down in front of me without any clothes on."

7. *Sex for revenge.* A wife and husband can punish each other by each being unresponsive to the approaches of the other. Adultery often has as its chief purpose to avenge oneself upon one's spouse. Sadistic behavior and rape often have both revenge and domination as ends. The thought behind the behavior is "I'll show you! I'll get even!"

8. *Sex as proof of abnormality.* A plea of abnormality can be used to justify evasion of many challenges in life. One

of my young patients told me, "I am a masturbator. How could any girl possibly be interested in me?" He avoided contact with girls and behaved very shyly when in their company on any occasion. Another patient was convinced that he was abnormal when he experienced homosexual desires. He actually only experienced such desires when he was annoyed for some other reason (particularly when he had failed to make a sale to a client). Being abnormal was something to worry about; therefore, he would stop working for the day and spend his time worrying about himself. When he could see that all these thoughts were a device to excuse himself from working and that he rebelled against working when he could not have his own way, the homosexual thoughts "miraculously" disappeared.

If one is tone deaf, one is excused from playing the piano; if one has a bad memory, one does not have to remember obligations. By the same token, one can produce some entertaining or horrifying sexual ideas or feelings in order to prove that one is defective and cannot be expected to function in ordinary ways.

Summary

From a teleological point of view, most sexual behavior can be assessed in terms of the private purpose of the person employed in it. This permits a psychological point of view that yet takes full account of an ethical system of values. Sexual behavior can be classified as useful or useless, depending upon whether the purpose is socially useful or socially useless. The latter is either openly destructive in consequences or fails to lead to satisfactory and meaningful sexual activity. Neurotic and sociopathic sexual symptoms all seem to be examples of *abuses* rather *uses* of sex. Such a value system can probably be useful to all counselors, clergy as well as members of the other healing profession.

ORGAN INFERIORITY
and
PSYCHIATRIC DISORDERS IN CHILDHOOD *

The Theory of Organ Inferiority and Psychic Compensation

In 1907 Alfred Adler, then still a member of Freud's circle, published a set of observations and deductions which were intended to draw a close connection between constitutional deficiency and personality structure.[1] (Organ Inferiority and its Psychical Compensations) According to Adler, the latter could provide a "psychic compensation" for the former, in line with the hypothesis of biologic compensation, in which one part takes over some of the function of another defective part of the body.

Among the many clinical examples in his monograph, Adler offers the example of Ladislaus, an 8 year old boy, who, while playing with a schoolmate was injured in the left eye with the point of a pen. Two months later, Ladislaus again needed medical care for a foreign body in the same eye. Two months after this, he received another injury in the left eye, again from the point of a pen wielded by another schoolmate. The patient on examination was found to have hypermetropia and lacked the conjunctival reflex in both eyes. The family of the patient showed a surprising amount of eye problems. A younger brother had hypermetropia and convergent strabismus. His mother had these two and, in addition, diminished visual acuity. The mother's brother suffered from convergent strabismus and conjunctival eczema, while the maternal grandfather had a history of diabetic iritis. Is this not more than coincidence Adler asks; is it not a familial organ inferiority of the eyes, which manifests itself in various ways?

---

* Reprinted from *Pathogenesis of Nervous and Mental Diseases in Children,* edited by Ernest Harms. New York, 1968. Published by Libra Publishers.

Adler describes the following characteristics of organ inferiority:

1. It is a morphologic aberration, a functional disturbance or a relative weakness (weakness which appears only under physiological stress).

2. It occurs in an organ, an organ system, an embryological segment or a primitive layer.

3. It is inherited or acquired during early development.

4. Since it is a "defect," it compels "compensation" in accord with the biological laws of homeostasis and survival.

5. The clinical manifestations are:
   a. Morphologic abnormalities such as abnormal size of the organ or stigmata of degeneration.
   b. Functional abnormalities such as underactivity, compensatory overactivity or signs that organs physiologically linked to the inferior organ are compensating for it.
   c. The inferior organ or system acts as a *locus minoris resistantia* both physically and mentally.
   d. Psychic signs of compensation shown by a heightened inner attention and concentration on the inferiority which may even lead to a "high development" of the organ, both training it and capitalizing on it through the organism's capacity for adaptation and variability.

Adler does not explain further how psychic compensation occurs, but goes on to offer more clinical examples both from his own experience and from well known examples; thus Beethoven was deaf, Mozart had a deformed ear and Bruchner had a nevus under the zygomatic arch, supposedly indicating an inferiority which had a segmental arrangement. All three were prominent musicians. Many other examples of well known individuals who hypercompensated for inferiorities are described by Rey.[3]

Nolan Lewis,[2] in discussing Adler's theory says that for Adler "organ inferiority" represented a defect in the material available for the construction of a normal well-balanced personality pattern. This defect became a "point of crystallization" *(locus minoris resisantia)* for the mental superstructure of compensation and hypercompensation. Moreover, it tended to increase the feeling of inferiority experienced by every child during the process of growth and acculturation. It could become an obstacle or even be converted into an asset (hypercompensation).

In 1907, Adler was deterministic in his psychological thinking. An organ inferiority required organismic compensation in accord with mechanistic biological laws and that was definite. Much psychological behavior, such as choice of vocation, temperament, the existence of neurosis, etc., was the outcome of the striving to compensate for such a defect. Three years later his thinking had changed,[4] and he introduced the ideas of "striving for superiority" and "inferiority feeling." The "striving for superiority" replaced the biologic law of compensation as the determining motivation in human behavior and the "inferiority feeling" was the subjective conviction of deficiency, the feeling of not being good enough or capable enough, which spurred the individual on toward "upward striving," sometimes in a healthy *direction, sometimes not. Thus, the individual's own opinion of himself determined how hard he would strive and his opinion of where his best chance for growth and development lay would influence the direction of his endeavors.* Modern Adlerian theory does not hold that organ inferiorities have a direct deterministic effect on the personality of the individual. It is the *conviction of inferiority,* the *inferiority feeling* that is important. Thus, if a red-headed child thinks that red hair is a defect, he acts as if he needs to compensate for it. On the other hand, a pretty little girl may achieve so much importance and praise for her looks that she may concentrate her attention exclusively on her appearance and even base all her upward striving on it, so that it is *as if* she had an organ inferiority. Her prettiness becomes her psychological "point of crystallization" or *locus minoris resistantia.*

Thus, in latter day Adlerian theory, an organ inferiority becomes a *possible* stimulus for psychic compensation if it is subjectively perceived as a defect or obstacle. The subjective perception of a defect and the subjective conviction that it is important to compensate for the defect are required before the child initiates a psychic compensation. For example, children hold differing opinions about the status of childhood. Some children will not like being smaller than adults, will consider it a disadvantage and will try to hasten the process of growing up by acting "big" or otherwise imitating adult traits. Other children are not eager to grow up, feeling that their smallness gives them special privilege and freedom from responsibility. Thus, small size, may or may not be perceived as a defect. In some parts of the world obese women are considered desirable; in our country a slim figure is more highly valued. Thus environment and culture play a definite role in determining how a person will view his own body and whether or not it will please him. Ex: A 6 year old boy required glasses for myopia. Both parents and an aunt wore glasses for the same condition. The boy was rather proud of the glasses since they made him feel more grown up. Not evaluating myopia as a defect, he had no need for psychic compensation.

Psychic Compensation and Psychiatric Disorder

Much psychic compensation is in a healthy direction. When a spastic child develops strong intellectual interests, when a homely girl trains herself to be charming and pleasant, when a physically weak boy becomes a diplomatic persuader of others, we all recognize that the child is compensating for a deficiency along courageous and useful channels.

Neither is all psychiatric disorder in children the consequence of unhealthy psychic compensation. Much of what we call behavior disorders in childhood are situational disturbances between a child and a parent, child and teacher, or reactions to perceived rejection, unhealthy ways of striving for attention, fear of being hurt by others, insecurity about one's place, feelings of defeat, fear of failure, and/or fear of one's own hostility or badness. None of this behavior requires an organ inferiority as a cause; they can be disturbances in the personal relations and mental life of children with completely normal constitutions.

When, then, is psychic compensation associated with psychiatric disorder? It arises only when the child is of the opinion that the perceived inferiority is too great an obstacle for him to overcome by a useful and constructive path and he therefore becomes discouraged. He then gives up and is left with a strong conviction of his own deficiency in the face of life or else he seeks concealment, subterfuge, special advantage or other safeguarding devices in attempts to avoid the consequences of being deficient.

Ex: A 15 year old boy with congenital deafness and consequent imperfect speech prided himself on his skill at athletics, chess and argument as compensation for his defect. He was a very poor loser in any contest, usually refusing to admit defeat. His behavior conveyed the impression: "I know more than you, I understand things better than you and you are wrong if you think you have defeated me." Unfortunately, he had alienated his friends by his dogmatic attitude and excessive argument but refused to admit that this had happened. Instead, he developed obsessive doubts and fears which prevented him from engaging in athletic and social activities, preferring the safeguard of obsessive symptoms to the painful admission of his own defeat in his endeavors.

The amount of courage and optimism in the child is important for determining his reaction to the organ inferiority and the direction of his compensation. The pampered, overprotected and dependent child will feel inadequate to face the rigors of life even under the best of conditions; he will feel more so if he perceived himself the owner of a deficiency. Ex: A nine year old boy had congenital clubfoot and wore a special shoe. He was the only child of doting parents, and his mother was overprotective and overindulgent. From his relationship with his mother he developed the idea that he needed the service and admiration of others. He suffered from a painful fear of engaging in any athletic activities, especially swimming. One time, in a swimming class in school, the students were required to lie on a table to demonstrate how well they could perform a certain stroke. The patient became very embarrassed and afraid to expose his deficiency. He feared he might be laughed at because of his deformed foot and would never again feel the equal of his classmates. The experience remained as a painful memory for over 15 years.

Such neurotic symptoms display the child's discouragement, which is focused on the deficient organ. The child assumes that the deficiency places him at an unalterable disadvantage and he must sidestep the "stresses" that life puts before him.

Sometimes the child may be making relatively adequate compensation but still perceives himself as deficient and again becomes discouraged and develops a reactive psychiatric disorder.

Ex.: A 10 year old boy with mild amyotonia had been a happy, friendly child. The parents, aware of the diagnosis from the first year of life had encouraged the child to be interested in activities which required fine motor coordination and little strength rather than gross motor activity and muscle power. He was slow in walking, running and riding a bicycle but was able to build electronic appliances requiring considerable skill. His first setback came when he was nine at the time that competitive athletics were started in his school. After a few weeks his classmates discovered that he was slow and clumsy on the ball field and not only teased him but forcefully rejected him. The school rules required that he participate, so the teacher always put him on one of the teams. His teammates were abusive and complaining. He became, in a few months, an irritable, complaining, unfriendly child who was only appeased when he could have his own way. He began to do poorly in his studies and to constantly quarrel with a younger sister who was a popular child with normal muscular development. He felt disliked and unwanted, becoming reactively critical and fault finding with others to the extent that it was apparent to all that he was an unhappy child.

Organ Inferiority of the Central Nervous System and Psychiatric Disorder

The study of psychiatric disorders in brain-damaged children shows no clear correlation between brain damage and personality structure. Shere[5] studied thirty pairs of twins in which one twin was spastic and concluded that there was no "spastic" or "athetoid" personality and that spastic children frequently fulfilled the criteria of mental health better than the non-spastic twin. This is contrary to the view sometimes expressed that various types of cerebral palsy have typical personalities.

Gingras, et al, also studied twin sets with one spastic member and found that the presence or absence of "neurotic traits" depended more on parental behavior than upon physical inferiority. This is further presumptive evidence that the "feeling of inferiority" is more related to the child's status within the family than to the existence of an "organ inferiority."

However, brain damage may also produce mild to severe mental incapacitation, which may be manifest as mental retardation and/or hyperactivity, destructiveness, emotional lability, poor self-control and poor social adjustment. When a neuropsychiatric symptom is the direct result of a neurologic lesion, the organ inferiority theory does not apply. However, the child's reactions to his own damaged brain would be related to his inner perception and attitudes and to how he views his place and what compensation he assumes is necessary. Much of the brain-damaged child's dependency and anxiety is associated with his tendency to feel helpless and inadequate and can therefore be considered a psychic compensation .

The retarded child is subject to severe stress when he is challenged to keep up with his peers in school, or when a younger sibling outstrips him in accomplishment. Thirty cases of mental retardation with brain damage were subjected to clinical observation and psychological testing. They were unselected cases from a child development clinic drawing its clientele from an economically deprived population. Almost all the children had "adjustment problems" and none were considered well-adjusted. However, among the symptoms they manifested only the symptom of hyperactivity was present in most cases. The children showed a great variety of behavior corresponding to the varieties found in physically intact children. Some were dependent and timid, some bold and forward, some demanding and spoiled, some guarded and defensive. One acted the "big shot," another was withdrawn. Such "character" symptoms are more likely to be evidence of particular personality types than of brain damage. We are therefore tempted to conclude that unless a psychiatric symptom is a direct consequence of disturbed neurological function, it is the result of a personality disturbance. Personality structure may be influenced by the existence of a damaged organ (the more the damage the more likely the influence), but is more directly influenced by the existence of damaged self-esteem or mistaken claims and aspirations in the child. Brain damage and/or mental retardation may act as discouragers of the child and in this way be a detriment to his personality development. Therefore, items such as parental attitudes, sibling relations, peer relations, etc. seem ultimately more important in influencing personality than the existence of a defect.

Other Organ Inferiorities and Psychiatric Disorder (the "use" of an organ)

There is no good evidence that any physical deficiency needs to be accompanied by psychiatric disorders. However, there are some forms of physical illness in which psychic components play a large role. This group of conditions includes asthma, various skin diseases and ulcerative colitis. While it is generally agreed that emotional stress is frequently a precipitating cause and the cause of relapses or recurrences, physical stress can also precipitate these conditions and there has never been satisfactory evidence that emotional stress or a particular type of personality are a *sine qua non* for these illnesses. It is more reasonable to assume that these illnesses are indicative of organ inferiority and are experienced by the child as a serious defect. The child may then develop certain personality traits as compensatory devices, such as sensitivity, dependency, and anxiety. Such traits frequently result in the child's inhibition in expressing aggressive interpersonal feelings, such as has been noted in ulcerative colitis by Prugh.[7]

The existence of such physical illnesses which are closely intertwined with neuro-humoral mechanisms can set into motion the "organ inferiority leads to compensation" sequence. Thus, the child focuses his attention and interest upon the abnormality and may capitalize on it in two ways:

1) He may use the abnormality as a rationale for evading situations or tasks in which he anticipates failure or for demanding special service and consideration from others (especially the parents).

2) He may use the disturbed function to express his inner feelings *(organ jargon).* In this way, the sensitized organ speaks his mind for him and the increase in disturbance is an attempt (usually unconscious) to communicate a message to others (such as a call for help in the asthmatic attack) or convey a retort (such as the "you have defecated upon me, therefore I defecate back on you" hidden idea frequently seen in ulcerative colitis.) This ability to capitalize psychologically on a physical defect (and make an "asset" out of it) is no different than the use of any other asset or talent in line with one's private motives.

Since the organ inferiority has by this time become a very important component of the child's personality structure, psychiatric treatment and careful mental hygiene may be required to assist the medical treatment of the illness. Strictly speaking, the psychiatric treatment is not directed toward the physical condition itself but toward the correction of unfortunate personality traits in the child and mistaken attitudes and child-rearing practices on the part of the parents.

Organ Inferiority and Diagnostic Categories

It is obvious that a constitutional defect is acting as a direct cause of psychiatric disorder in the acute and chronic brain syndromes and in the mental retardations. In some of the psychophysiologic reactions, as has been discussed, an organ can be used for a psychologic purpose. The choice of the organ probably depends on several factors, but organ inferiority with consequent heightened attention to the organ could certainly be one of these factors. In the functional psychoses of childhood it has been suggested by some[8] that there exists an inherent defect of the CNS, but definite proof is still awaited. This brings us to the neuroses, behavior disorders and specific symptom reactions of childhood, none of which requires an organ inferiority for their existence, but in any of which it may be a predisposing cause.

Certainly, an anxiety reaction, or a phobic reaction in the child needs no preceding organ inferiority. However, a *feeling of inferiority*, in some manifestation (sometimes called feeling of anxiety, guilt, shame etc,) seems always found in these and other neurotic conditions. In this state, as in the other behavior disturbances, the personality of the child and the psychological stress he experiences are the main determinants.

There are however, a certain group of special symptom reactions which sometimes occur without other easily visible signs of mental disturbance and seem to fit in many ways the concept of an organ inferiority. This group includes conditions such as stuttering, enuresis and learning disability.
Ex.: An 11-year-old boy had never been entirely free from nocturnal bed-wetting. Pediatric studies revealed no abnormalities. At the age of 18 months, he had sustained an *inguinal hernia,* apparently after trying to lift a heavy object. At 2 years the hernia had been successfully repaired. Psychological examination indicated that the child felt very self-conscious about the enuresis and was discouraged about his ability to overcome it. There was no demonstrable psychological reasons for the enuresis. There were some mild indications that he could benefit from psychiatric treatment, and psychotherapy was begun. Some aspects of the child's personality and behavior improved, but the enuresis persisted. At this time, a local urological consultant examined him using a new technique for radiographic visualization of the bladder and found a "funnel-shaped bladder" that was unable to retain the larger amount of fluid required to prevent nocturnal urination. In addition, a mild urethitis was causing a certain amount of urgency so that the bladder evacuation occurred before the child could arouse himself. Ephedrine sulfate at bedtime was prescribed for the child, and the enuresis stopped.

Naturally, this was not a psychiatric disorder, though on its way to becoming one. However, the existence of the bladder defect, the urethritis and the history of inguinal hernia would all fit the concept of an inferiority of the urogenital tract.

Many cases of enuresis respond well to psychological treatment, possibly because maturation itself is so important in establishing bladder control. How much enuresis can actually be traced to organ inferiority remains a moot point.

In the half-dozen cases of stuttering treated by us, the children were repressed and self-repressing, not daring to voice their inner resentments, yet feeling very resentful. Since some of these children were actually afraid that strong feelings would lead to destructive behavior and consequent punishment, these even tried to train themselves not to have strong feelings about anything.

If a child strongly fears his own rebellious impulses and if he holds the conviction that words have magic powers: Ex: (the primitive belief in the power of a curse or in the name of God) then the psychological background for the symptom of stuttering is established. However, not all such children stutter. Is the difference a defect in the speech organs or their nervous connections? Or is the child more likely to stutter when it is a more effective way of coping more with the repressing parent? A parent who values proper speech very highly is likely to pay excessive attention to the speech of the child. This in itself is sometimes enough to encourage the child to stutter (just as urging a child to eat may diminish his appetite). It is for this reason that in the treatment of stuttering in a young child it is so important to help the parents be less anxious about the child's speech, not fuss over it and become purposely slightly deaf when the child stutters so that the symptom loses its power to stimulate the parent and the child hopefully learns to use clearer speech for communication.

Thus the question of whether or not an organ inferiority exists in the special symptom reaction is a complicated one. Perhaps the best answer is that organ inferiority is a frequent predisposing cause but is not a necessary cause.

Treatment of Psychiatric Disorders Associated with Organ Inferiority

Psychiatric treatment of children whose emotional problems seem closely connected with an organ inferiority does not seem to call for any special or unusual procedures. However, it seems useful in a review such as this to also examine the goals of such treatment:

1. When a physical disability interferes with the child's normal development, good mental hygiene requires us to:

   a. try to prevent the child from developing the conviction that the defect is an insuperable obstacle to a useful and happy life;

   b. Try to keep the child from believing that the defect makes him less desirable or less significant as a member of the human race;

   c. encourage the parents to accept the child as he is. The study of Shere[5] showed that CP children who were accepted by their parents were more likely to make good adjustments. This was true even when the parents only acted "accepting" and repressed tendencies to reject the child.

2. Since visible defects frequently influence the child's acceptibility of his peers, he needs to be encouraged in the development of such assets as will win acceptability from others, such as intellectual pursuits in the physically handicapped child, etc. It is a mistake to impress the child with the danger of being rejected by others when they discover the defect.

   Example: A woman with chronic eczema had been told by her mother all through her childhood that she should never let her father see her in the morning before she had applied her masking ointment. She had grown up with the conviction that she could never marry because she could never let a man see how she looked.

3. In order to help forestall feelings of inferiority and discouragement, the child may need special training in a compensatory activity. A child with legs damaged by polio may still become a swimmer and thus achieve physical skills and abilities. Such a child needs the experience of success, or he may need special training in the use of the organ itself; e.g., special therapy for the stutterer.

4. Some defects are amenable to repair, such as deformed ears or jaw which may be corrected by plastic surgery. This is an important part of the overall treatment of the child.

5. When the child is already using a defect as an excuse for avoiding required tasks or for requiring special privileges, he is striving to turn his handicap into an asset by using neurotic mechanisms, just as he might use a functional symptom as a neurotic claim for special consideration. Some children even exaggerate a defect to excite attention and sympathy. The trick of walking with a limp to arouse interest has been tried by many children. The treatment is now that of the neurotic problem itself.

Summary

An organ inferiority is a constitutional defect that provokes compensatory development according to biologic laws. The compensation may take place in the psychic life as well as in the body according to the hypothesis of holism, the organismic unity of the individual. There is no inevitable psychological consequence of a physical defect. Functional psychiatric disorders require the prior existence of psychological stress, which depends on the particular personality structure of the child. When the child experiences an organ inferiority as personally injurious to his development, his acceptability and his worthwhileness as a human being (feelings of inferiority), this in itself constitutes a psychic stress and may provoke psychiatric disorder. The particular type of psychiatric disorder provoked, need have no relation to the type of organ inferiority. It is possible however, that childhood schizophrenia and infantile autism may contain a CNS defect in its etiologic background. Psychophysiologic conditions are probably associated with an organ inferiority, while in the case of the specific symptom reactions the question of organ inferiority as a predisposing cause is complicated and must be individually answered for the individual case.

REFERENCES

1. Adler, Alfred, *Study of Organ Inferiority and Its Psychical Compensation*. New York, 1917.

2. Lewis, Nolan, in the Forword to Adler, Alfred, *Study of Organ Inferiority and Its Psychical Compensation*. New York, 1917.

3. Rey, Marie Benyon. *The Importance of Feeling Inferior*. New York, 1957.

4. Adler, A. *Der psychische Hermaphroditismus im Leben und in der Neurose. Fortschritte der Medizin* 28, 1910. Also in Ansbacher, H. & Ansbacher, R. *The Individual Psychology of Alfred Adler*, N.Y., 1956.

5. Shere, Marie Orr. "Socio-emotional factors in families of the twin with cerebral palsy." *Exceptional Children*. 22, 5, 1956.

6. Gingras, G., Lemreux, R. et al. "Twins and cerebral palsy; a combined study." *Acta Genetical Medicae et Gemellogiae*. 7, 2, 1958.

7. Prugh, D. G. "Influence of emotional factors on clinical course of ulcerative colitis in children." *Gastroenterology* 18, 1951.

8. Bakwin, H. "Early Development of Children with Schizophrenia." *J. of Ped.* 43: 1953.

9. Bender, L. "Childhood Schizophrenia." *Amer. J. Orthopsychiat.* 19, 1949.

10. Kallman, F. S. "Schizophrenia" in *Heredity in Health and Mental Disorder*. New York, 1953.

PSYCHOLOGICAL DISTURBANCES WHICH INTERFERE WITH THE PATIENT'S COOPERATION *

The doctor-patient relationship is of a complex social nature with the role of each party more or less defined by cultural traditions. Historically, the doctor is seen as a powerful healer with esoteric knowledge who advises, counsels and prescribes. The patient is a supplicant who enters into a specific kind of transaction with the doctor in order to receive the desired help. The traditional script calls for the doctor and patient to meet in office, home or hospital, where the doctor conducts an examination and prescribes or administers treatment. The patient's role calls for him to follow the expert advice and submit to the treatment.

What actually happens between doctor and patient is often a complicated modification of this classical script. One important complicating factor is the tendency of many patients to feel personally threatened by the role they are supposed to play. Because of perceived "dangers" they do not easily cooperate as patients, are not open and honest with the doctor, do not follow his advice or prescribed treatment and use various kinds of defensive maneuvers to ward off the anticipated danger. Some of these maneuvers are conscious devices; that is, the patient is fully aware of what he is doing. In many cases, however, the patient is not aware of the real meaning of his behavior; that is, he doesn't realize that he feels threatened, or what the threat is or that he is engaged in defending himself.

Such dangers are perceived threats to the patient's self-esteem (people have to live with themselves) or to his "plans" for dealing with the doctor and other people (we all have some secrets we'd like to keep private).

* Reprinted from Psychosomatics, Volume V, Pages 213-220, July-August, 1964.

Dangers Perceived by Patients

The kinds of dangers perceived by patients can be categorized under the following headings:

1. *The Danger of Being Defective.*—Some people are afraid they won't make the grade; that they will not be able to live up to the requirements and expectations of life, or to their own standards for themselves. A patient may even fear a physical examination because he sees it as a test which he may fail. He may rebel when referred for psychiatric consultation because he believes only "abnormal" people go to psychiatrists; or he may feel that any intelligent person ought to be able to use his "will power" and straighten himself out.

> One girl could not stand to be examined physically. She had one breast that was small and underdeveloped and perceived this as a great deformity that would keep any man from wanting her. She was afraid the examiner would make a comment about the breast and "make her feel bad."

2. *The Danger of Being Exposed.*—Many people have nagging feelings of inferiority. They cannot allow others into their innermost thoughts and cannot be spontaneous lest they betray themselves. A doctor is not only a healer, he may also be seen as an investigator and a judge who must be kept at a safe distance.

> A husband will sometimes not be willing to come see a doctor who is treating his wife because he is carrying on a clandestine affair and has some suspicion that this is connected with the wife's complaints. If he comes, he often lies freely. A malingerer also fears exposure.

3. *The Danger of Incurring Disapproval or Enmity.* Some people are so dependent on the good will of others that they fear disapproval. They feel it necessary to please the doctor or even want to be "liked" by him. In order to avoid disapproval they may avoid giving information that may annoy the doctor or will suffer in silence rather than complain. Thus they may lie about their food intake, use of drugs, social misbehavior, et cetera. The same behavior can be found in people who are afraid of being hurt in their relationship to others. The patient, not really trusting people, may feel that the doctor must be appeased and flattered, as one may deal with

a powerful authority. Such behavior is more common among people who have been brought up in a rigid authoritarian atmosphere and who have had to develop devices for dealing with domineering people to avoid antagonizing them.

4. *The Danger of Being Ridiculed.*—It is surprising how many patients will not report certain symptoms or thoughts because they are afraid that others will laugh at them. They are usually adherents of the "intelligent people ought to be able to help themselves" school. They will not report fears which they label as "childish," such as persistent fear of the dark, or rituals associated with eating, sleeping, bathing, sexual behavior, et cetera. They are usually also afraid to report their private fantasies and secret aspirations for the same reason. Such behavior becomes more dangerous when the patient, out of his fear of being ridiculed or criticized, fails to report symptoms which would be important in making a diagnosis.

> An 18-year-old girl suffered from dizzy spells and headaches but did not tell her parents because they had always ridiculed any of her complaints. When the symptom of generalized edema occurred, the parents accused her of being pregnant. A sympathetic employer arranged for medical examination. An adrenal tumor was found and surgery was advised. The parents, members of a religious cult, refused to agree. The girl did not feel able to withstand such parental pressure and discontinued further medical care.

5. *The Danger of Being Taken Advantage Of.*—There are times when the doctor-patient relationship requires that patient submit to the doctor's prescriptions and ministrations. For some people, the physician is such a superhuman figure that it is relatively easy for them to submit to his power and to trust him. There are others who do not have such high opinions of the medical profession and who worry about the doctor's integrity; whether he will charge them too much; whether they really need the prescribed treatment, et cetera. Some people distrust others as a general principle and prefer to keep their distance.

6. *The Danger of Not Getting Necessary Help.*—Given a completely free choice a patient usually chooses a physician

in whose judgment he has confidence; but some patients cannot easily have confidence in anyone. Some can only develop confidence slowly and need to know the doctor a long time before they can trust him. Pessimistic and discouraged people, especially, will doubt that they can really be helped; they tend to give up easily if the doctor's advice does not bring some immediate benefit. Some people cannot tolerate uncertainty and will not be happy until the doctor finds a "cause" which explains their symptoms, so that treatment can be instituted immediately. In this group fall those patients who do not like to leave the doctor's office empty handed. They want an injection or a prescription as concrete evidence that they are getting help.

7. *The Danger of Submitting to Order.*—There are a few strong-willed individuals, so determined to have their own way, that they refuse to submit to any order or schedule other than their own. Safety, for them, lies in defeating the schedules of others; they act as if the doctor's prescriptions were an imposition on them. They will not take prescribed medication because they "don't want to get used to pills." They will not follow diets, *et cetera,* and want to dictate to the doctor the terms of their own treatment; finding some fault or other with the doctor's suggestions. They need to feel "in control." An example is the patient who says, "I want you to x-ray me," whether this test is indicated or not in the doctor's judgment. Such a person tends to use the phrase, "I want . . . " with unusual frequency.

8. *The Danger of Having to Face Responsibility.*—Life asks all people to face various responsibilities at various times. Many psychogenic disturbances are precipitated when a person's courage fails him in the face of a responsibility. Some people even feel unable to assume the responsibility for taking good care of themselves. Others will not face their obligations to a sick member of the family; or if they contribute to that person's distress, will not accept the obligation to stop doing so. The girl who has studied singing for many years does not have the courage to give a concert. A woman does not feel able to face the responsibility for caring for

a newborn child. A man feels unable to meet the requirements of marriage and a family. All such demands may
tempt the person to look for an escape in illness or elsewhere.
Even a kindly physician's advice may seem too hard to follow
to the person who feels appalled at any task that requires
courage.

9. *The Danger of Having to Face Unpleasant Consequences.*
—Illness can sometimes provide a way out of difficulties for the
person in a stressful life situation, but most of the time it is
an unpleasant experience. Restrictions, painful suffering,
disabilities and the approach of death are generally dreaded
events. Some people prefer to "play ostrich" rather than face
dangers. Others are excessively fearful and habitually anticipate dire consequences in every situation. Thus, a headache
always means a brain tumor, a pain means cancer and a pal-
pitation means heart disease. Even firm reassurance from the
physician only allays their fears temporarily. These patients
want to feel that "everything is all right." They may even
delay coming for examination because they dread finding out
that something is wrong, or dread a painful experience. Thus,
some patients put off a visit to the dentist. Others nurse and
self-medicate a symptom for a long time before coming for
help.

All the above "dangers" are threats to the patient's image
of himself and may interfere with his relationship to the
doctor. The "dangers" are that he may look bad, feel bad,
have to account for his deficiencies and/or misbehavior and
be confronted with himself as he is and with the demands
of the situation. In these situations he is pessimistic, lacks
courage and has little confidence in himself and/or the doctor.

Defensive Patterns Used by Patients

The "defenses" are forms of behavior used to ward off
the dangers. Some defenses will be brought into play only
occasionally at a time of stress. Others are used almost
constantly because the individual is running away from some
of the obligations of living and needs to constantly excuse
himself from them. ("I can't work because I get nervous and
my stomach hurts.")

If the defenses are to be effective they must either be able to save one's self-esteem when it is endangered or somehow entrap, mislead, neutralize or defeat the doctor when he threatens.

These defenses can be categorized as follows:

1. *Externalization*[1] ("the fault lies outside of me").—Man tends to populate the world with moral values since he apperceives it in the dimension *good-bad*. Things, situations, and like matters have a plus or minus value or are neutral. One consequence of this is the concept of "fault," "blame" or "guilt." Some people are raised in an atmosphere of "blaming," and nothing for them ever happens accidently or fortuitously; it is always someone's "fault."

Externalization preserves self-esteem and relieves one of responsibility by employing a false hypothesis which can then be developed by logic into a justification for one's own failures. At its best, it removes the stigma of failure and places it elsewhere, by using the concept of "guilt" or "blame." Everything that happens is "caused"; therefore, anything which is bad or wrong has its source in some bad or wrong "cause." The individual is simply the victim of this circumstance and has no choice but to act the way he does.

There are several varieties of externalization.

(a) *Cynicism* ("life is at fault").—The cynic relieves himself of responsibility by disparaging life, present circumstances or people. He may excuse himself from political responsibility by claiming that all government is in the hands of "bosses." He may excuse his economic irresponsibility by depreciating the "system." Since in his opinion people are only out to get what they can from each other, he too is entitled to get as much as he can. Virtue for its own sake does not exist for him; it always has an ulterior motive. Thus, all life is a meaningless struggle; the only things that may count are pleasure and the ability to avoid falling into the world's traps.

---

[1] For this term and several of the following, the author is indebted to Karen Horney. See *Our Inner Conflicts,* New York, Norton, 1946, Chaps. 7 and 8.

These people, often disillusioned idealists, are actually quite discouraged about life. They show the same tendency to disparage the physician in his attempts to help them. They are given to making statements such as: "It's nature that heals; the most the doctor can do is help nature along a bit"; "I don't believe in pills"; "You're just saying that because you're trying to make me feel better"; "My cousin had psychiatric treatment for four years and he's just as sick as ever"; "Are you sure it isn't just my change of life"; "I've heard that once you have this kind of operation you're never the same again." Each such remark treats the doctor as if he were trying to put something over on the patient and therefore deserved a challenge.

(b) *Inadequacy* ("I'm just an innocent victim").—Whereas cynicism requires disparagement, inadequacy requires a demonstration of *incapacity*. The *incapacity* makes the patient an innocent victim of bad circumstances and excuses any real failures or defeats the *threatening demands of others*. In effect, the patient says, "It's not me that's at fault, it's my defect."

(1) Sickness is perhaps the most common excuse used for retreating from life; it is relatively acceptable in most cultures. If one is sick, one is obviously incapacitated and should be excused from demands. This defense is used consciously by children to avoid school and by adults to avoid work ("My nerves keep me from working").

(2) *A bad background* can also be used to plead for special consideration. One person may claim he never had a chance in life because he comes from a broken home; another may excuse himself because he never had enough education; a third will blame friends for misleading him; a fourth (more psychologically sophisticated) will lay his failures at the door of an overprotective mother; a fifth will find some body defect which makes ordinary living too hard for him.

If the physician makes a demand upon such patients, they often become worse, as if to convince the doctor they are too unreliable or weak to fulfill his demands. Characteristically, they hope the doctor has a magical solution that sets the world straight for them again. They tend to avoid facing their own obligations to *do* something to improve their situation.

(3) Some people offer for an excuse that they are victims of their own cravings and impulses. The alcoholic may state that everything would be fine if he could just stay away from whiskey. The obese patient will claim he has no "will power" to avoid overeating. A patient may claim that he has "irresistible impulses" or strong sexual cravings. Another will say "I have a terrible temper" as if temper were something which possessed him in spite of himself.

(4) A special variety of victim is infrequently found in our culture. This is the person who feels possessed by a demon or supernatural force. He is therefore not responsible for his behavior.

(c) *Rebellion* ("I can't afford to submit to life").—Some people who use externalization see themselves in a perpetual battle with life. The main issue for them is who will win and who will lose. They have developed tactics for defeating the rules. They refuse to submit to ordinary schedules, they will not accept restrictions, they will not permit themselves to be persuaded by argument and will defeat the efforts of the physician unless these efforts suit their own purposes. In chronic illnesses requiring prolonged treatment, the rebel is constantly in trouble with the doctor. Some of them use alcoholism as an expression of the rebellion ("nobody can stop me from drinking"). Because of his loose living habits, he may contract tuberculosis and then refuse to hold still for treatment. He feels duty bound to oppose instructions to rest, stop smoking, appear regularly for examination or otherwise follow orders. (One such woman with intermittent claudication was instructed to stop smoking and found that her desire to smoke increased thereafter.) Under additional stress, the rebel may become aggressive and openly paranoid, but at most times he is troublesome to the people around him because he is so honor bound to resist them. The cynic disparages; the rebel defeats. In his antagonistic behavior he attacks what he thinks is to "blame" for his problems.

(d) *Projection* ("It's all their fault").—In the paranoid, one can see the most extensive development of the use of "blame" to exonerate oneself and implicate another. The tactics are to accuse another of evil intent and machination (feelings of persecution). This may become a delusional system and may be accompanied by heightened feelings of self-importance (delusions of grandeur). One man, struggling to be economically successful and sensing that his business projects were going to fail, distracted himself from the approaching failure by finding fault with his wife, blaming her for not helping him and not being considerate enough. Eventually he accused her of being in love with someone else. Under such circumstances, no one could blame him for being too upset to concentrate on his business. Furthermore, business success becomes less important when one's marriage is in danger. The person who uses projection need not always "believe" in his accusation. It is sometimes enough just to have strong suspicions which can be used as a device for explaining a failure.

A special variety of projection still seen in certain subcultures is the idea of being "spellbound." Here the victim feels put under a spell by a malevolent person. This person is sometimes a "witch," a "hypnotist" or someone similar.

2. *Blind Spots* ("If I don't look at it, it will go away").—Some people try to deal with problems by refusing to face them. A parent will refuse to believe that a child is retarded. An ardent suitor will not admit that his beloved does not care for him. An alcoholic will not face the long term consequence of his drinking. This kind of person lets things go until they become catastrophes. He may ignore his bodily symptoms, warning from his boss or even the leaky roof on his house until the roof caves in. His tactic is to *overlook*. If a problem is not seen, no action is called for, no strong feelings are provoked, no alerting signals are heard. One can maintain the illusion that danger is far away. If he sees and hears no evil, he can continue to believe it is not there.

3. *Excessive Self-control* ("I will not let anything upset me").—To be strong, impervious and brave is a cultural ideal. In militant cultures, such an ideal seems especially important. The story of Muncius the Roman who burned his

own hand to show his determination; the Spartan boy who let the stolen fox gnaw at his vitals; the stories of the Sioux Indians who were impassive in the face of pain; all of these express the importance of *self-control*. Emotions, pleasant or unpleasant, are strongly suppressed. The sensation of one's power lies in the ability to control one's *own feelings*. This ability is sometimes quite helpful. It permits a patient to endure considerable manipulation by a surgeon or dentist without requiring anesthesia.

If such tendencies to control feelings are excessive they lead to inability to feel the normal emotions such as anger, joy, sympathy or love when appropriate. Sometimes, such a person goes through his life like an automaton, performing all the appropriate actions though devoid of feeling; being relatively safe both from sorrows and ecstasies.

4. *Arbitrary Rightness* ("My mind is made up; don't confuse me with facts").—Another way of resolving problems is to make an arbitrary decision and permit no doubts. When doubt has been eliminated and one is sure about what is right, the necessary course of action is obvious. Unfortunately, proper medical care often calls for the patient to accept the facts as the doctor sees them. Patients with preconceived notions about the causes and cures of their diseases waste the doctor's time, try his patience and frequently try to dictate their own treatment. Sometimes, such a patient will not even listen to what the doctor has to say, because he is so busy telling the doctor his own opinions.

5. *Elusiveness and Confusion* ("Don't pin me down").— A favorite defense of children against adults is "I don't know" or "I don't remember." *Elusiveness* is also used by the schizophrenic when he does not wish to be understood. It is used by the lover whose ardor is cooling when his inamorata brings up the subject of marriage. The hysteric is more likely to use *confusion*. He claims not to understand what the therapist is driving at, forgets readily, becomes confused and pleads inability. Both these tactics prevent a direct confrontation by avoiding all obligations. Indeed when the

hysteric is confronted with a direct dynamic interpretation of his symptom, he often stops having this particular symptom and switches to another one.

It is sometimes remarkably difficult to get a good clinical history from the person who uses this defense. The patient may give such a confusing account of his illness that one is unsure of chronology, sequence, relationship to other factors or even of what the patient's exact complaint happens to be. Lying, bluffing and changing the subject are other varieties of this maneuver. When successful, it effectively conceals from the doctor the real motivation of the patient's behavior.

6. *Retreat* ("Nothing ventured, nothing lost").—The patient who finds his doctor too threatening can defend himself by not returning. The man who fears the obligations of marriage may simply avoid such involvement. In essence, retreating is an attempt to solve problems by removing oneself from the problem area. The retreater will often not make the obvious move to solve his problem. The physician may urge him to take some action; to change his job, move out of his parent's home, go back to school for more education, engage in more social activities, et cetera. All such tasks require taking a chance on oneself; something the retreater is unwilling to do. He will often restrict his field of action to only those areas where he is certain of his ability to avoid what he fears. Into other areas he simply does not enter.

7. *Contrition and Self Disparagement ("mea culpa")*.— Whoever uses this tactic is pretending to blame himself. His breast beating is actually insincere though he himself is usually not aware of this. Self-disparagement serves to forestall attack or punishment. (Sometimes it is even used as a way of asking for compliments; as when one's wife says, "My hair is really a mess, isn't it dear?") This method includes feelings of guilt and expressions of sorrow. Such guilt feelings, no matter how subjectively painful they are, are excuses and apologies. They usually permit the person to continue the misbehavior and continue to feel guilty about it. The self-disparager frequently uses the phrase "I'm sorry." If a stronger defense is required, he can elaborate this phrase;

e.g., "You have no idea how terrible I feel; I'm really very, very unhappy about what I did."

I have a good friend who uses these tactics at the bridge table. When he makes a mistake and his wife begins to criticize him, he acts as if he were disgusted with himself. He says "How could I have done such a stupid thing?", grimaces and looks quite unhappy. His wife's expression changes from criticism to concern and she becomes supportive; saying, "It wasn't so bad," etc.

(a) *Good intentions* ("I didn't mean it").—Good intentions are often used together with *self-disparagement*. We learn as children, that our misbehavior is always less heinous if it was unintentional. We also learn that words may speak louder than action; therefore we often manage to say something and do another and get away with it. The tactics thus require a loud claim that one really had his heart in the right place and should be forgiven for all misdeeds, because they were accidental, unintentional and actually contrary to one's wishes.

The physician may accept the patient's contrition as a sign that he has changed and will often be disappointed. Confronted with the patient who uses this defense, the physician is advised to understand his behavior according to the rule that actions speak louder than words; in this light, regrets are vain unless accompanied by changes in action. Indeed, the person who is truly contrite and intends to change, spends almost no time in feeling guilty; he busies himself with bringing about the changes.

8. *Suffering* ("I feel bad").—Pain and sorrow, common to us all, produce ready sympathies. This provides suffering with certain positive social values. The person who uses suffering as a defense feels entitled to make certain demands.

(a) *Suffering as manipulation* ("If you don't do what I want, I'll die and then you'll be sorry").—Sometimes, a symptom is useful to the patient because it influences the behavior of others. A wife's anxiety attacks may keep her husband home at night, a child's tears may keep the parent from punishing him, a headache may evoke solicitous concern.

The goal desired may be much more important than the suffering itself which is perceived as incidental and a small price to pay, or appears inevitable anyhow; i.e., the sufferer doesn't feel he can avoid it—the others must try to help him feel better.

(b) *Suffering as justification* ("I have a right to my own way. Look how much I suffer when I don't get it").— This kind of patient is usually regarded as emotionally unstable" or "over-sensitive." When something distresses or annoys him, he suffers. He reacts to unpleasantness with the feeling "I can't *stand* it." At times he only wants to be spared obligations; at other times he resents any restriction of his way of living. He feels entitled to avoid whatever causes him suffering and so he suffers whenever he is faced with a situation he dislikes.

(c) *Suffering as self-glorification* ("The amount of my suffering proves my nobility").—Martyrdom is an acceptable way of achieving status and suffering confers merit on the sufferer in many eyes. Wounds suffered on the battlefield are marks of distinction. Byron's clubfoot made him more romantic. Therefore, the person who uses this tactic will elaborate, exaggerate and focus on the suffering. His *"welt-schmerz"* will be deeper, his pains more intense, his outrage greater. He is attracted to situations in which he can be hurt, prefers to complain rather than take preventive action and when one bad situation is over, he will find another. He is a little like the person who sits in the bathroom complaining of the odor but neglects to open the window.

The physician encounters difficulties in his treatment of such a patient. He may be pressured by incessant demands for medication or for privileges. The patient may frequently ask for relief from the suffering but will not want to stop doing what produces the suffering. When the physician fails to satisfy the patient, the latter may develop many symptoms which are *directed against* the former as a reproach ("Your treatment is making me worse instead of better"). Furthermore, the physician who fails to "appreciate" the suffering is accused of being callous and heartless.

9. *Sideshows* ("I can't take care of anything else until I have slain this dragon").—One way of avoiding activities in the main tent of life is to become occupied with a sideshow. A hobby can be a useful relaxation; but when carried to excess it becomes an obsessive interest that interferes with other activities. The student who dislikes homework, procrastinates by finding "busy work" that occupies his time. A person who is bored may devote his thoughts to pleasant fantasies. The wife who fears or resents intercourse, becomes preoccupied with her husband's faults in order to keep him at a distance. The miser uses a preoccupation with money as justification for retreating from obligations or challenges. A hypochondriac uses his body sensations for the same reason. Some hysterical symptoms such as fear of hypodermic injections, excessive modesty or inability to produce a urine specimen, are petty annoyances. It is more serious when a patient avoids necessary surgical procedures as a result of his fear. However, the symptom is often a dramatic sideshow which obscures the main issue.

> A 36-year-old wife and mother complained of abdominal pains, headaches and dizziness. The symptoms started a year earlier after her father died and she began to think about bringing her invalid mother to live with her. She had not yet done so because she wanted "first to be all well again" in order to properly care for mother.

A phobia can also be a sideshow, which appears most conveniently as a defensive device against a threatening situation, driving attention away from the actual problem.

Cancerophobia, syphilophobia and the obsessive fear of heart disease are examples of symptoms which are difficult for the physician to dispel because they usually conceal a conflict in the life situation. If faced with death or serious illness, one feels entitled to neglect other social obligations.

Furthermore, such symptoms are sometimes used to compel someone else to comply with a wish.

> A 21-year-old woman, newly a mother, did not feel up to the obligation of caring for her infant on her own. She became frightened if left alone by her husband, developed obsessive thoughts that he would be killed while driving to work and became so upset each morning that the husband had to stay home from work for

a month. Each day as soon as she saw he was not leaving for work, her anxiety subsided until evening when she began to prepare herself for the unconscious strategy of the following morning.

Obsessions and compulsions are sideshows *par excellence.* The obsessive creates an "imaginary dragon" and spends his time trying to slay it. For example, a mother says "I keep thinking I'll pick up the knife and stab the baby." This is interpreted by some as a hostile unconscious wish to destroy the baby. It is much more likely to be a sideshow which is dramatic and frightening but obscures the real problem. Concerned with such horrible thoughts, other problems become small by comparison.

10. *Rationalization* ("I didn't really fail").—Rationalization is the use of logic to deceive oneself. It is a common basis for the other defenses, especially for externalization, arbitrary rightness and blind spots. It provides an intellectual "explanation" of what has happened or is happening in such a way that self-esteem is preserved and the exhibition of good intentions remains intact. The scheme provides a face-saving explanation of why it happened, how it was unavoidable, that it was actually right, that it was natural, that everyone else would have done the same thing, that after all it was not so bad, et cetera.

A versatile patient can use many different defensive strategies to reinforce his attitudes and "justify" his behavior.

One young man who had no confidence in his masculinity and avoided women, engaged in a dialectic with his therapist over a period of several months before he finally decided to take a chance on marriage. To begin with, he was convinced that girls could not possibly like him, that they would instinctively avoid him, that he was bound to make a bad impression, et cetera.

A girl, newly employed in the office where he worked, began to try to attract his attention. In spite of his fears, he found himself attracted to her. She went out of her way to be nice to him, but he insisted that her behavior had no significance; that she was "just being nice to everyone" (blind spot).

As the weeks went by, her little attentions continued. He protected himself by saying, "She doesn't know me yet, when she finds out more about me, she won't like me" (self disparagement). A short while later, he concluded that she must have an ulterior motive, "She must want me to help her with her work, or something" (cynicism). However, the girl persisted and he began to relax in her company, even flirting with her. He considered asking her out for a date, but decided he would not take the chance of being turned down (retreat).

She finally suggested a date and he felt he had to agree. He came to his therapist in a near panic with the idea, "I'll be too sick to go out with her" (inadequacy). He returned from the date pleasantly surprised that they had both had a good time, but insisted, "It was just lucky, next time I'll mess it up" (rationalization). Their relationship continued and he began dating her often. He began to talk of marriage, but insisted that one could not marry on his salary (arbitrary rightness), that most marriages are unhappy (cynicism) and that he was "too neurotic" for marriage (inadequacy). However, he admitted that he was happier than he had ever been before and hopeful they would remain together. He began to develop attacks of giddiness on the street (sideshows) and insisted that he could not marry until "all his problems were cleared up."

By this time, the therapist had discussed the situation with his girl friend. She hoped to marry him and was advised to be patient. The patient was confronted with his avoidance maneuvers and became disgusted with himself and critical of his behavior (contrition). One day he offered the following excuse: "There must be something wrong with her otherwise she wouldn't put up with a neurotic like me" (projection).

Shortly after this, he insisted that he didn't know if he should give her up or continue to see her, saying "I can't make up my mind what I want. A man who isn't sure what he wants has no right to take up a girl's time" (confusion and self-disparagement).

One by one, his strategies were interpreted to him and his underlying assumptions exposed and questioned. Nine months after they met, they became engaged. After a few happy weeks he became more irritable and depressed. His fiancee was ready to break the engagement, but he had already progressed so far, it appeared reasonably certain he would overcome this stumbling block too. The patient became apathetic, losing interest in the girl and the forthcoming marriage (retreat). He admitted his "cold feet" but saw no way of backing out. At this point he was shown how he had always been the rejector of girls rather than rejected; that he had always kept his distance from them, not they from him. He was informed that he could still crawl back to his lonely shell and stop relating to the opposite sex. He responded with a dramatic recovery from the depression and went ahead with the marriage.

By now, they have been married four years and are the parents of one child. The marriage seems a happy one.

Summary

The ordinary physician-patient relationship is often disturbed by the patient's fears of exposure, being hurt, being taken advantage of or otherwise being placed in an unpleasant situation. At such times the patient is not willing to follow the rules for being a patient, that is, he will conceal information, refuse to follow advice, insist on his own ideas, or otherwise defeat the doctor's efforts to help him. Various defensive patterns of behavior are used by people who wish to protect themselves against many of life's demands or obligations or to excuse their own behavior. These same patterns are used by the patient to protect himself against the physician and the demands of the doctor-patient situation.

VARIOUS PURPOSES OF SYMPTOMS*

In medicine, a symptom is a condition that accompanies or results from a disease and serves as an aid to the diagnosis of such disease. The concept that a symptom may have a purpose is familiar to medicine. For example, the purpose of diarrhea is to expel the irritant from the digestive tract; of pain to signify that something is wrong; of a cough, to remove foreign material from the trachea.

Alfred Adler made the basic assumption that "We cannot think, feel, will or act without the perception of some goal" (1, p.3) . He considered the following statement an important proposition of Individual Psychology: "Every psychic phenomenon, if it is to give us any understanding of a person, can only be grasped and understood if regarded as a preparation for some goal" (1, p. 4). A psychic symptom, like any other psychic phenomenon, has a purpose and can best be understood if its purpose is understood.

It is sometimes easier to see symptoms as reactive behavior than as purposive. To illustrate, anxiety can be seen as a reaction to a perceived danger; depression, as a reaction to discouragement. However, in cases where such reactions are exaggerated or overly prolonged or inappropriate, this point of view does not give a clue to their understanding.

Freud's point of view was that "A symptom is a sign and a substitute for an instinctual gratification which has remained in abeyance; it is a consequence of the process of repression" (6, p. 20). "Sometimes the symptoms become valuable to the ego because they obtain for it, not certain advantages, but a narcissistic gratification which it would otherwise forego." Thus the obsessional uses his symptoms to feel "better than others because he is specially cleanly or

* Reprinted by permission from *Journal of Individual Psychology*, 1967, 23, 79-87.

specially conscientious." Freud calls this the epinosic or secondary gain of the neurosis (6, p. 36). Thus, Freud also recognized that symptoms have a value to the patient, but he preferred to see them primarily as compromises with the instincts, and only secondarily as purposive.

In the eyes of the Individual Psychologist, the main significance of the symptom lies in its service to the individual in striving for his goal. Adler, in discussions of clinical examples, frequently mentioned the purpose or "secret intent" in the use of the symptoms. Thus, a symptom is described as the means of securing a triumph, of retiring from danger, of reproaching another, of creating the fiction of a superiority (1, pp. 11-13), of providing an exemption from the demands of reality (1, p. 23); "to force his environment into his service" (1, p. 38); "compelling [others] to concern themselves continuously with him" (1, p. 55).

Adler's views were presented more systematically by the Ansbachers. In one chapter his writings on the function of the neurotic symptoms are organized (2, pp. 263-280). All symptoms are seen as serving as safeguards for self-esteem, or as excuses. One way to accomplish this is through aggression, specifically through: depreciation of others, as in sexual perversion; accusation of others for imagined faults, etc.; and self-accusation and neurotic guilt.

Another way of safeguarding is through "distance" for which four categories are recognized: "moving backward" which includes suicide, agoraphobia, compulsive blushing, migraine, anorexia nervosa, etc.; "standing still" as in psychic impotence, psychogenic asthma, anxiety attacks, compulsions, etc.; "hesitation and back-and-forth" as in all methods of killing time such as procrastination, compulsions, pathological pedantry; and "construction of obstacles," primarily psychosomatic symptoms.

Adler sees the symptom as an expression which is always in accord with the patient's life style, his basic attitudes toward life. Physical symptoms show the same expressiveness. Thus, vomiting may say, "I can't swallow that," abdominal cramps and rumbling in the bowels, "My bowels are in an uproar," and so on. Such organ jargon (2, pp. 222-225, 308-310) frequently provides the clue to the underlying purpose of the symptom.

To return to the above category of aggression, many symptoms can be regarded as offensive weapons. "Neurosis is the weapon of the coward and the weak" (2, p. 269). Thus, one way the Individual Psychologist tries to understand a symptom is to ask himself against whom or what the symptom is directed. For example, the depressed patient expresses his antagonism to the life situation in his negative feelings (3), the paranoid symptoms destroy logic (9), the hyperactive child annoys his mother (5), the frigid woman rejects a man's power to arouse her, the homosexual negates the sexual value of the opposite sex (7), and the emotionally unstable person punishes those who fail to accede to his demands by making a scene.

Returning to the category of distance, it is a truism of Individual Psychology that neurosis is an evasion of life tasks and neurotic symptoms are evasive devices. "The neurotic has always collected some more or less plausible reasons to justify his escape from the challenge of life, but he does not realize what he is doing" (2, p. 332). The neurasthenic, for example, uses his various sensations to announce to himself his incapability of meeting this or that unpleasant situation (4). Symptoms become part of an overall strategy dictated by the dominant goal, fitting into it in many different ways and serving many purposes.

This paper proposes to spell out further the Adlerian concept of the purpose of the symptom by listing various stratagems which have been most commonly found in patients examined by the authors.

Safety Stratagem

Some symptoms are intended to insure against failure, exposure, or other catastrophies (2, pp. 263-266). The symptom may have the effect of making it impossible for the patient to meet an onerous responsibility, or at least to delay the "moment of truth" (cf. the various methods of safeguarding through distance described above). He may use the symptom to disqualify himself from a race he does not wish to run.

A 37-year-old bachelor suffered from sexual impotence only with a pretty 33-year-old divorcee who wanted to marry him. He never was impotent with prostitutes or in casual affairs. This was the first girl he really considered marrying. However, he felt he could not propose in view of his sexual inadequacy. When he was asked what he would do if the symptom were not present (2, p. 332), he answered, "Why, I'd get married of course." His dreams and early memories revealed an antagonism toward and fear of close relationships with women.

The symptom of mild depression sometimes has the purpose of safeguarding the person from the demands of an occupation or a life situation that requires some action he is unwilling to take or some commitment he is unwilling to make.

A single man of 30 was alternately a successful salesman and a poor one. He would become enthusiastic and work steadily for several months, then become neurasthenic and depressed and spend several weeks frittering his time away. He also complained that he wanted to get married but would not undertake the responsibility of a family because he could not be sure that he would work steadily. A dream revealed the underlying dynamics and showed his fear of commitment to any particular job or relationship. He dreamed that he was on a battlefield and all about him were men fighting with each other. Corpses were strewn about the field and he was lying quietly, pretending to be dead. He felt himself in the midst of a heroic struggle but had no feeling of belonging to any particular side in the conflict. He had no weapons and wondered if he were supposed to be a combatant. He would have liked to have taken part in the struggle, but felt that to move would be to betray himself and invite the attack of others. He waited until night came and crept away to a safer place.

A special instance of the safety stratagem is "buying double insurance." This device is the opposite of the double bind. It is a double unbind. No matter what the outcome, the safety of the individual is secured and therefore he can afford to take a partial chance. Inability to concentrate on school studies often falls in this category. The real problem consists in the fact that the student dares not make a true test of his intellectual capacity. His symptoms insure him against the failure of being of ordinary intellect.

A student is overambitious and demands of himself that he be "on top." He cannot really afford to take the chance that his best efforts may leave him in the average range of his class. At first he makes resolutions to study and indeed fantasies that he will study exceedingly well and do much outside reading on his subject. But somehow he rarely sits down actually to do the necessary work. In a few weeks he is already behind and the chances that he will do exceedingly well are already poor. Now he feels disappointed in himself and even less inclined to study. People who want to be "on top" have no interest in studying hard to achieve only an average passing grade. This is shown in his procrastination, inability to concentrate, and restlessness when he sits down to his books. Throughout this comedy the student maintains his feeling of intellectual superiority. He blames his trouble with studying and his poor grades on bad habits, "nervousness," lack of discipline, dull teachers, and uninteresting courses. He consoles himself with the thought that his is really a bright intellect that is merely unproductive for the moment, that if only he were able to study properly, he would be at the top of the class. If he should happen to get a high grade in spite of the fact that he did not study, that is all to the good. He may even boast, "I never opened a book." If he receives a poor grade, it is not because he is stupid, but because he was "lazy," and in our society most people would prefer to be regarded as lazy rather than stupid (2, p. 391; 8).

The following is another example of the way in which a symptom is used to "buy double insurance." Once a psychiatrist (Rudolf Dreikurs) mentioned in a talk that neurotic symptoms were often used to evade responsibility. After the talk, a member of the audience introduced himself and stated that he suffered from headaches for which no organic cause had ever been found, but that the headaches were not used by him to evade his responsibilities. The man was indeed a successful playwright whose works were well known. "I seldom let my headaches keep me from working," he said, "I will simply go ahead with whatever I have to do in spite of pain." The psychiatrist confessed this case was perhaps an exception. They chatted a few moments longer about plays and authors and the playwright turned to go. As he left, he said, "Just think what I could have done had I not had these headaches. Who knows? People might have compared me with Shakespeare."

Hero-Martyr-Saint Stratagem

An efficient, capable individual will sometimes complain of distressing symptoms even when no overt stress is apparent. He may create his symptoms in order to demonstrate his strength, just as some with saintly aspirations create temptations in order to demonstrate their virtue by not succumbing, or the aspiring martyr arranges to suffer in order to demonstrate his moral superiority over his tormentors.

A medical student complained that he became panicky and felt faint during conferences and ward rounds. He feared that his supervisors would ask him questions which he would not be able to answer. He did not have such symptoms during written examinations. Furthermore, in his ward work he made a good record. He developed a reputation for skill in drawing blood and was called upon whenever his colleagues could not find a vein. He felt a sense of triumph at these times. He enjoyed examining new patients and was exhilarated by a diagnostic problem. He recognized that he was happier when faced with a challenge. He could not understand his emotional symptoms and felt like a coward and weakling for having them.

One can guess that this man found unpleasant any situation in which his superiority was questioned. Furthermore, his way of being superior was to be a hero, to accomplish what others could not. A situation which did not provide him with an obstacle to overcome had no value for him. At the conference and ward rounds, he not only had no chance to act the hero, he was even in danger of being exposed as someone who did not know as much as he should.

What then is the purpose of his symptoms? They supply him with a challenge and an obstacle and therefore, as Adler says, with a chance to enhance himself (2, pp. 275-276). At each conference he again has the chance to be a hero by struggling with and overcoming his spurious weakness.

Attention-Service-Love Stratagem

The purpose of some symptoms is obviously to get something. Sometimes it is sympathy, sometimes service, but always in this case it is to make oneself the center of the field of action through the symptom. For example, if a mother pays more pleasant attention to the child when he is sick and tends to ignore him when he is not complaining, it becomes most tempting to the child to complain about some body discomfort in order to win the mother's attention. Symptoms used for this purpose work better if they have some dramatic quality which compels the attention of the observer.

A 22-year-old girl was seeing a therapist weekly for an anxiety reaction. For several consecutive Sunday nights she experienced a panic and telephoned her therapist. On one such occasion the therapist asked, "Why is it that you become panicky every Sunday night and don't seem to have this trouble at other times?" "Well," she answered, "I know you're at home on Sunday night." The therapist confronted her with the purpose of her panic; namely, to give her an excuse to call him at a time he was known to be available. The Sunday night panics subsequently stopped.

Power Stratagem: Manipulation of Others

The most direct example of a symptom which has as its purpose to overpower is the temper tantrum (2, p. 227). The small child with temper tantrums kicks, screams and holds his breath until the parents give in, acknowledging his power. The hysteric throws a fit when someone is displeasing her. The mother who wants to hold on to her adult son develops chest discomfort and shortness of breath when he becomes interested in a marriageable girl. The symptom is designed to overpower the others and permit the sufferer to have his own way. In effect, the patient is saying, "If you don't do what I want, I will suffer and *make* you do it." "Tears and complaints—the means which I have called 'water power'—can be an extremely useful weapon for . . . reducing others to a condition of slavery" (2, p. 288).

Revenge and Retribution

There are times when a symptom has the purpose of destructive retaliation against a person or life situation (3, pp. 269-271). Patients who use symptoms for revenge are usually very discouraged people who have lost the hope of dealing with the situation constructively. In taking revenge, they are striking back in anger, willing to do damage because all is lost anyway. Adler gives an example of a depressed woman who dominated her husband and who developed a guilt complex over an affair she had had 25 years before with another man. By confessing to her husband and accusing herself she could continue to torture him (2, p. 272).

A 17-year-old girl, in a state hospital with a diagnosis of emotionally unstable personality and history of rejection and neglect by her parents, was a problem to the hospital staff for two reasons: she impulsively broke windows with the back of

128

her hand, and she mutilated herself by putting sharp foreign objects in her ears and under her skin. She was well treated in the hospital and given considerable attention since the staff appreciated the extent of her early emotional deprivation. But whether she had privileges or not made no difference in her behavior. On visits to her family she behaved the same way. Under questioning she said that she broke windows to "get even." She wanted to get even with her family and a life situation that kept her a patient in a mental hospital. If she wanted something and did not get it, if her mother's visit had irritated her, or if she had for any reason begun to brood on her lot, she became impulsively angry and broke whatever windows she could reach. She injured herself for the same reason.

Face-Saving Stratagem

Sometimes a symptom has as its purpose to repair damaged self-esteem. The development of a delusional system in the later stages of schizophrenia is often an example of this. Another common example is guilt feelings. When a person has done something he believes is wrong, feeling guilty about his behavior is sometimes his way of salving his own conscience and consoling himself that he is really a well-intentioned person (2, pp. 272-273).

A 3-year-old girl was observed to sneak to the cookie jar, take out a cookie and eat it. She then slapped her hand and said, "Bad girl." Having made "retribution" she then took more cookies, repeating the self-reproach after each one (5).

Other face-saving devices include the development of symptoms which excuse or mitigate a failure (2, pp. 265-266). Thus, a man who lost his job because he dropped and broke a valuable instrument developed a tremor of the hands. He reported that he lost his job because of his "shakes," not because of incompetence.

Creating Excitement

Sometimes a symptom has the purpose of creating a furor and agitating others. The symptom may be directed against a particular person the patient wants to annoy or sometimes against a life situation that is boring and uneventful. The excitement may be generated internally or externally. The former is often the purpose of irrational impulses.

A young law student complained of strange impulses to jump down from heights. He would experience these impulses upon crossing bridges or looking down at the ground from windows in tall buildings. He did not believe that he would give in to the impulses but was annoyed by them and was concerned lest they be symptomatic of an approaching mental disorder. The patient could not seem to relate his symptoms to any particular problems. There seemed to be no critical situation in his life. But the symptoms never appeared when he was busy, under stress of work or school, or otherwise occupied. He experienced them only when he had no immediate task to perform, when he was for the moment idle, bored or forced to wait for events. The symptoms were used by him to keep his life interesting and exciting.

Some people find exciting and dramatic the recital of illnesses, operations and doctor's examinations. Hypochondriacal symptoms (which are often somatic pre-occupations) often make life more exciting.

The creation of external excitement is quite clear when the symptom is a fainting spell or perhaps a hysterical fit. Contagious forms of hysterical behavior, such as mass swooning of young female audiences of popular singers, fit into the category.

A man of 40 went to a management consultant with the complaint that he could not organize his business well. He had a wife, a mistress, engaged in casual affairs, ran two businesses, became constantly involved in community projects and seemed willing to give himself to any new challenge that came his way. When a friend became ill with cancer, he contacted specialists in other cities to ask their advice. He took up the cause of better housing for Negroes. He drove his car at excessive speeds. He encouraged his mistress to date other men and became obsessively jealous when she did. Because of his numerous activities he was a poor family man and erratic provider. In spite of his positive accomplishments, he was much more impressed by the atmosphere of confusion and excitement in which he lived. He recounted his exploits gleefully, dramatizing his narrow escapes and his inability to live a stable life. The excitement actually meant more to him than anything else. A narrow escape afforded more pleasure than a constructive achievement. He scarcely solved one problem before he was embroiled in another.

Proof Stratagem

Some symptoms have the purpose of the patient strengthening his position, of proving to himself that his judgments are correct and thus defeating the logic of those who disagree with him. These individuals "run after their slaps in the face" (2, p. 290). The paranoid may deliberately provoke others to behave badly to him in order to gather evidence that others are unfair to him. "Lack of joy in life, the continuous expectation of accidents, . . . superstitious fear, . . . distrust" and other manifestations of oversensitivity lead to the repetition of unpleasant experiences and the lack of pleasant ones (2, p. 290).

> A 14-year-old boy, subject to much deprecatory criticism from his father, was pessimistically convinced of his own inadequacy. He did not believe that psychotherapy could ever help him. He had originally come with a complaint of pain in the left side which was diagnosed as psychogenic. After several months in treatment, he had long since stopped talking about the pain and complained about numerous other symptoms. One day, as he complained about the ineffectiveness of therapy, the therapist pointed out that at least he no longer had the pain in his side. The patient demurred and changed the subject. When he returned the following week, he gleefully reported that the pain in the side had recurred. This was additional proof that psychotherapy could not help him.

Keeping a Symptom in Reserve

Patients who respond favorably to psychotherapy sometimes retain one or two symptoms for no readily apparent reason. They seem to be functioning well, are happy, and report a feeling of progress. They sometimes feel that some particular problem has not yet been worked out and feel that they therefore need more treatment. The reason for such behavior is sometimes that the patient does not dare to become completely well. He prefers to keep a symptom or two in reserve just in case he may need them. In this way he maintains a form of insurance against future difficulties, keeps himself in training by practicing the symptom, and avoids a complete commitment to the idea that he is now completely well and no longer has excuses for holding back in life. As one patient said when he was confronted with the meaning of his behavior, "After all, nobody can ever get *that* well."

Summary

The purposive nature of the symptom is stressed by Individual Psychologists in accordance with their point of view that behavior is goal-directed, and that the functional mental illnesses represent inadequate or socially useless ways of dealing with the demands of life which arouse in the individual fear of failure. The authors have described some purposes of symptoms found with relative frequency among patients in psychotherapy.

REFERENCES

1. Adler, A. *The practice and theory of Individual Psychology* (1920). Totowa, N.J.: Littlefield, Adams, 1959.

2. Adler, A. *The Individual Psychology of Alfred Adler.* Edited by H. L. & Rowena R. Ansbacher. New York: Basic Books, 1956.

3. Adler, K. A. Depression in the light of Adlerian psychology. *J. Indiv. Psychol.,* 1961, 17, 56-67.

4. Dreikurs, R. The problem of neurasthenia. *Int. J. Indiv. Psychol.,* 1936, 2 (3), 14-34.

5. Dreikurs, R. Guilt feelings as an excuse. *Indiv. Psychol. Bull.,* 1950, 8, 12-21.

6. Freud, S. *Inhibitions, symptoms and anxiety* (1926). London: Hogarth, 1949.

7. Krausz, E. O. Homosexuality as neurosis. *Int. J. Indiv. Psychol.,* 1935, 1 (1), 30-40.

8. Lindgren, H. C. *Psychology of personal and social adjustment.* New York: American Book, 1959.

9. Shulman, B. H. An Adlerian view of the Schreber case. *J. Indiv. Psychol.,* 1959, 15, 180-192.

THE MEANING OF PEOPLE
To The Schizophrenic
versus
The Manic-Depressive *

Almost all schools of psychopathology view schizophrenic and manic-depressive disorders as having different underlying psychodynamics. Yet the line of demarcation between the two psychoses is sometimes indistinct. An individual may carry a diagnosis of manic-depressive reaction through several hospitalizations before he is diagnosed as schizophrenic, because now he may show considerable disturbance of perception in the form of hallucinations and delusions.

This paper purports to explain some of the similarities and especially differences in the clinical features of these two disorders on the basis of life style. The term life style was used by Adler to denote the unity of the individual including his self-image, his personal biased apperception of the world, his private logic, his evaluation of the environment, his self-ideal or final goal, and his characteristic patterns of response.

Similarities in Life Styles

The life styles of schizophrenic and manic-depressive or cyclothymic patients are alike in at least three respects. They are characterized by (a) extremely low self-esteem, (b) extremely high-flown goals in life, and (c) drastic measures for narrowing the gap between the self-image and the self-ideal (1, 2, 3). The psychosis in each case, is an unconstructive attempt to narrow this gap. This attempt is doomed to failure because it represents a decision to evade a challenge which, however, remains to confront the evader as a constant accusation that he is not what he claims to be.

___

* Reprinted by permission from *Journal of Individual Psychology*, 1962, 18, 151-156.

Differences in Life Styles

The essential difference in the life styles in the two psychoses is in the form of relatedness to others, although both are deficient in social interest. People mean different things to the schizophrenic and to the cyclothymic. This is the main argument of the present paper.

The schizophrenic has little hope of getting along with people. Others are hostile, alien, and enemies, or at best unsatisfactory people to do business with. His aloneness is a protection against the disappointing transactions with others. He prefers to keep people at a distance and pushes them away.

The cyclothymic has no hope of getting along *without* people. Others may be hostile, but they are not alien. They may be enemies, in which case they must be defeated, coerced, persuaded or given-in to, in order to do business with them because relating to others is a *sine qua non* for existence. He wants people around him and tries to suck them in, dominate them if he can, control them.

The high-flown goal of the schizophrenic betrays a less people-centered quality. To be perfect, or godlike, or super-man, or never to make a mistake are schizophrenic types of self-ideals. A schizophrenic would rather be aloof from conventional aspirations. He prefers to destroy the world as it is and remake it closer to his heart's desire.

The cyclothymic ideal needs people for its fulfillment. It is something like: to be always liked by everyone, to be admired, to be constantly impressive, to be always loved, never to face disapproval, etc. A manic may set out to make a fortune, become a great lover, convert people to an idea about which he is enthusiastic. A person in the throes of depression bemoans his inability to perform the conventional tasks and achieve his conventional goals. He feels he should be smarter, more successful, more worthy of love and admiration. However, his *mea culpa* discloses a special social purpose: He is demanding the rightful place in the congregation which is given to those who confess and repent.

Thus, the symptoms of the schizophrenic push others away. The symptoms of the manic-depressive, though they sometimes backfire, are designed to keep others involved.

Childhood Development

If one reviews the childhood development in cases of the two psychoses, one is struck by an important difference in the life situation. The schizophrenic seems to have had no satisfying personal relationships with significant figures in his family. Even if the relationships started out well, in some way they became spoiled and disappointing (5).

The cyclothymic experienced pleasurable and satisfying relationships in childhood, at least to one person. The relationship may have had many disadvantages, may have been stormy, violent, punitive, and perhaps unpredictable. But it was perceived as satisfying, or at least potentially satisfying, and therefore was desired. The cyclothymic thinks he knows what a good human relationship is and hopes to achieve it some day.

One may say that in the cyclothymic the social tendencies were stimulated to develop at least to some extent, whereas in the schizophrenic the social tendencies were discouraged and inhibited.

This difference in childhood is also reflected in the marital and sexual lives of these two kinds of patients. This author recalls only two manic-depressives who never married, both women. Both had sexual affairs in which at least the sexual relationship itself was satisfying. One was too afraid of the responsibilities of adult womanhood to marry, and remained living with her family. The other was Caucasian and in love with a married Negro man who did not want to marry her. In both cases an attack of severe depression was precipitated when the sexual partner left the scene.

The author knows of many more schizophrenics who never married, some who never had any kind of sexual relationship, some who consorted only with prostitutes (which requires no emotional closeness), and at least two who carefully trained themselves to have no sexual feelings at all.

The Views of Jung and of Kretschmer

Our presentation begs comparison with the ideas of Jung and Kretschmer on this subject. Jung's "general attitude type" of introversion acts as though "an attempted ascendancy on the part of the object had to be continually frustrated." The extrovert, on the other hand, "affirms (the object's) importance. (His) subjective attitude is continually being oriented by, and related to the object. . . . for him. . . . therefore, its importance must always be paramount (6, p. 412). Jung states further: "The relation between subject and object, considered biologically, is always a relation of adaptation. . . . typical attitudes are therefore adaptation processes" (6, p. 414).

When other people are the objects of the relationship, the introvert must, then, destroy the power the other seems to have over him and prevent the other from successfully appealing to him or attracting him. (Therapists know how difficult it is to win the schizophrenic's full trust and cooperation). The extrovert, on the other hand, will exaggerate the importance of love, attention, the presence and the good opinion of others. Jung's general attitude types seem to support the opinion expressed in this paper, namely, that the schizoid (introvert) and cyclothymic (extrovert) have personality differences which include differences in their attitudes toward people.

Kretschmer described schizothymic and cyclothymic "temperaments" which are associated with leptosomic and pyknic physiques and therefore to a great extent inherited. These temperaments, which are present in normals, will influence the course of a psychosis if such a disorder occurs. Kretschmer describes the schizoids: "They seek . . . to avoid . . . stimulation from the outside, they close the shutters of their homes in order to lead a dream-life . . . They seek loneliness . . . in order to spin themselves in the silk of their own souls" (7, p. 161). He adds that their sociability is superficial, limited to a small closed circle or is non-existent. They have a "disinclination for human society." Cycloids, on the other hand, are described as sociable, warm. They "long for encouragement." Even when they keep it to themselves, they "have no antipathy toward human society" (7, p. 126).

Kretschmer's description of these "temperaments" sounds remarkably like Jung's description of the "general attitude types" and seems to support further the present author's conclusions.

Differences in Consensuality

These distinctions between schizophrenia and cyclothymia become more meaningful when we examine them with regard to consensuality or the syntaxic mode of experience. This is a concept introduced by H. S. Sullivan (8, pp. 28-29, 36) to denote that an individual's percepts about reality are used more or less in common by his society which requires a common language and common symbols for the purpose of communication. Consensuality according to Sullivan, is based on consensual validation.

If psychosis is defined as distortion of reality, then the schizophrenic and manic-depressive are equally "crazy." However, the schizophrenic, needing to "unrelate" to people (4), systematically destroys the bonds of communication and consensuality between himself and others. He develops a new language, creates a new world, ignores others, makes others ferocious enemies, or contemptible non-entities, and otherwise refuses to participate in a world which seems to have nothing to offer him. He cares not what the others do. This is why a person suffering from a schizophrenia will almost always seem more strange and more "insane" to the layman or to the less experienced therapists than will a manic-depressive. If many experienced therapists feel more comfortable with the former, that is because familiarity dispels strangeness and because these same therapists feel more pressimistic about their ability to understand and help the latter. Nevertheless, the schizophrenic seems more "crazy," more sick, more disorganized, and more "out of his mind" to most people. The manic-depressive, on the other hand, frequently seems rational. He does not misperceive so much, his behavior seems appropriate to his mood, and the experiences of grief or elation are familiar to all of us. His phenomenological world seems more like ours.

The explanation is that the manic-depressive must retain enough consensuality to understand others. He frequently fails truly to understand them, because he usually lacks empathy, the ability to put himself in others' shoes; but he desperately tries to. Also, he cannot afford to use neologisms, circumstantial speech, etc., because he dares not risk being misunderstood. Even when he does not respond verbally to questions (as in severe depressions), he is sending a non-verbal message that he wants and needs help, comfort, love, understanding, and support. He cannot discard the rules by which others perceive on pain of losing his relationship to others. No matter how disordered his affects become, he still remains "in contact." Indeed, if he were to give up all hope of finding his salvation in and through others, he could then discard the rest of his consensuality and become schizophrenic. This is perhaps the reason why a person may start out with cyclothymic personality traits and a manic-depressive psychosis and eventually become schizophrenic. Therefore, the manic-depressive seems understandable to the layman, while the schizophrenic seems strange and bizarre.

Summary

From the Adlerian viewpoint, schizophrenics and manic-depressives are alike in low self-esteem, high goals, and unconstructive means to narrow the distance between these two levels; they differ essentially in that the former have little hope of getting along with people, and the latter, none of getting along without them. Jung's description of extrovert and introvert, and Kretschmer's of schizothymic and cyclothymic support our differentiation. The use of Sullivan's concept of consensuality brings out further the difference between the two kinds of psychotics in their attitudes toward people, and explains why the schizophrenics seem more strange.

REFERENCES

1. Adler, A. Melancholia and paranoia (1914). In the *Practice and Theory of Individual Psychology*. Totowa, N.J.: Littlefield, Adams, 1959. Pp. 246-262.

2. Adler, K. A. Life style in schizophrenia. *J. Individ. Psychol.*, 1958, 14, 68-72.

3. Adler, K. A. Depression in the light of Individual Psychology. *J. Indiv. Psychol.*, 1961, 17, 56-67.

4. Artiss, K. L. *Symptom as communications in schizophrenia.* New York: Grune & Stratton, 1959.

5. Boatman, M. J. & Szurek, S. A. A clinical study of childhood schizophrenia. In D. D. Jackson (Ed.), *The etiology of schizophrenia.* New York: Basic Books, 1960. Pp. 389-440.

6. Jung, C. G. *Psychological types.* London: Kegan Paul, 1946.

7. Kretschmer, E. *Physique and character.* London: Kegan Paul, 1936.

8. Sullivan, H. S. *The interpersonal theory of psychiatry.* New York: Norton, 1953.

AN ADLERIAN VIEW OF THE SCHREBER CASE *

This is an attempt at an interpretation of the Schreber case from the Adlerian viewpoint, made possible by the recent translation of Schreber's *Memoirs* (18). The case has become famous in the history of psychopathology since it furnished the basis on which Freud presented his theory of paranoid schizophrenia (11).

Daniel Schreber, a jurist, stood as candidate for election to the German Reichstag in 1884. In 1885, he suffered an illness which was diagnosed as hypochondria. All we know about the illness is that it had no elements of the 'supernatural," i.e., there were seemingly no gross paranoid symptoms. After several months Schreber gradually recovered. In 1893 he became *Senatspraesident* of the court at Dresden (Chief Justice of the Supreme Court of Saxony). Several months after assuming his post, he again became ill. The details of this illness are described, from his point of view, in his *Memoirs,* published in 1903, a remarkable document. His descriptions are thorough, clear and perhaps chronologically correct; but his interpretations of the symptoms are, of course, the delusions of a psychotic. Chiefly he felt he was being forcibly transformed from a man into a woman ("unmanned"). He was "persecuted" first by his physician, Dr. Fleschig, later by God. Eventually he believed himself to be the Redeemer who, by becoming a woman, would save the world from evil that had taken place. Schreber's report includes a world-destruction delusion and shows his gradual paranoid reconstitution and partial reacceptance of (or return to) reality. Macalpine and Hunter (16), the translators and editors of the English edition, point out that Schreber had almost every symptom of paranoid schizophrenia. When he partly recovered, in 1901 or 1902, he was successful in having his rights restored to him by pleading his case well before the court. The court found him still insane but competent to manage his own financial and social affairs.

---

* Reprinted by permission from *Journal of Individual Psychology,* 1959, 15, 180-192.

According to Freud (11) the exciting cause of Schreber's illness was a passive homosexual wish for intimacy with or love from his physician, Dr. Fleschig. Why this wish appeared at this time was not known. The attraction for Fleschig was a feeling "transferred" from either Schreber's brother or father, or both. The homosexual impulse or fantasy was, however, unacceptable to Schreber. Thus an intense defensive struggle resulted which became manifest in the symptoms, especially the delusions.

Delusions of persecution to ward off a homosexual wish-fantasy are characteristic of paranoia. While social humiliation and slights are "prominent features," the main problem in paranoia is the homosexual component of the affective life.

The delusions of persecution were followed by delusions of grandeur. Schreber began to think of himself as a Redeemer, and of God (a father symbol) as his persecutor. The delusion of "being unmanned" (to be explained later) by God was more acceptable than "being unmanned" by Fleschig, and so Schreber found a more satisfactory paranoid solution to his paranoid dilemma.

The mechanism characteristic of paranoia is projection. The paranoiac is fixated at the narcissistic stage and has regressed from sublimated homosexuality back to narcissism. The precipitating cause of the breakdown is a frustration in personal relationships with either sex, accompanied by an intense wave of libido. As a result of the regression, the libidinal cathexes to the outside world are withdrawn. The internal catastrophe is projected, and the patient feels that the world has been destroyed. The delusions are, then, attempts to reconstitute the world, attempts at recovery. The fixing of the libido on the self results in megalomania.

These are the major items in Freud's theory of paranoia. He also discusses "dementia praecox" briefly, stating that there the point of fixation is earlier than in paranoia. The two conditions may occur together when there are two or more points of fixation.

Freud's theory of paranoia became so generally accepted by psychoanalysts that in 1940 Knight could write: "Perhaps no psychoanalytic theory of a psychosis rests on firmer foundations or has been less frequently attacked by critics of Freud" (14). Indeed, most psychoanalysts have either accepted Freud's position in all major points or have discussed the topic in terms of "object relations" (10). But even in wider psychiatric circles the view of paranoia advanced by Freud in his discussion of the Schreber case is regarded as if it were fully validated (17, p. 231).

How firm are these foundations? How well is Freud's view validated?

(a) Macalpine and Hunter accuse Freud of having selected from the available material only those parts which supported his contentions. Later studies generally did not go to the original source but merely re-examined Freud's one-sided selections. "All confirmatory studies of Freud's paper . . . are based exclusively on manipulating those parts of Schreber's memoirs which Freud extracted in order to prove his point" (16, p. 371). It is precisely in order to make a fresh interpretation from all the original Schreber data possible, that Macalpine and Hunter provided their translation of the *Memoirs*.[1] From an examination of these complete data Landis arrived at the conclusion: "Anyone who reads Schreber's *Memoirs* cannot help having doubts about Freud's interpretations of Schreber's experiences" (15).[2]

(b) New material has generally not confirmed the relationship between paranoia and homosexuality postulated by Freud. In a study of 80 cases diagnosed as paranoid schizophrenia Klein and Horwitz found: "The paranoid mechanism cannot be explained solely by homosexual conflict despite the convincing evidence of its pertinence in

---

[1] Macalpine and Hunter's own reinterpretation is in terms of a reactivation of unconscious, archaic procreation fantasies (16, p. 386).

[2] In this connection it is interesting to note that Freud ends the introduction to his analysis of the Schreber case with the request: "I would ask my readers to make themselves acquainted with the book by reading it through at least once beforehand" (11, p. 389).—Ed. note.

certain cases. It is so obvious in the cases in which it occurs, that the limits of its application are all the more surprising" (13). Dreikurs also found some paranoid schizophrenics who exhibited overt homosexual behavior and admitted homosexual desires, and points out that in such cases it is not possible to consider the delusions to be a defense against homosexual feelings (9).

Grauer (12) examined the Rorschach protocols of 31 paranoid schizophrenics for signs of homosexuality. Since the delusion was considered by Freud a defense against the appearance of the homosexual behavior, one should *not* expect more overt homosexuality in paranoid psychosis. Since the Rorschach is assumed to reveal unconscious phenomena on the basis of Freudian theory the hypothesis would appear justified that cases of paranoid schizophrenia should reveal more indices of homosexuality in their Rorschach protocols. Grauer found, however, no statistical difference in homosexual content between the records of paranoid patients and nonparanoid psychotics.

From such studies in general Walters concludes: "A very large discrepancy has been demonstrated between the generally accepted relationship and the quantitative studies of paranoia and homosexuality"; is was "the prestige of Freud's backing," rather than empirical fact, which "has continued to give his hypothesis a dominating role in the psychodynamic interpretation of paranoia" (20, p. 337, as reported in 17, p. 231).

Adler's Theory of Schizophrenia and Paranoia

Before offering our interpretation of the Schreber case an outline of Adler's theory of schizophrenia and paranoia would seem to be indicated.

Self-centered, high personal goal. Life style is the term eventually chosen by Adler to denote his conception of personality structure. Drawing particularly on Adler's later writings, Kurt Adler (8) characterizes the development of the schizophrenic life style as follows: The individual has a relatively great feeling of inferiority. By way of compensation for this, an extremely high goal emerges. To maintain such a goal in the face of reality requires special safeguarding devices. Increased self-centeredness is engendered which interferes with the development of social interest. The outside world is then seen as increasingly hostile and frustrating and the pre-schizophrenic withdraws from real life-problems which require cooperation for their solution. Failing to develop his social capacities and communication, he fails to develop common sense and logic which are social functions. Instead he develops a private logic in the service of his personal goal, and his fantasy increases. To maintain the idealized aggrandized picture of himself, he shifts the responsibility for his failure to solve his problems to the people around him, whom he already considers hostile. He commits himself to the apparent objectivity of the hallucinations and thus frees himself from responsibility for his condition. The schizophrenic despairs of ever being of significance in the real world. Alfred Adler considered hopelessness such an important element in the development of schizophrenia that he believed, "We could probably, by systematic discouragement, make any child into a person who behaved like a schizoid" (6, p. 46).

Regarding paranoia specifically, Adler listed twenty-three characteristics of the "paranoid attitude" (5). Briefly summarized, these are: The paranoid is fighting against a possible or anticipated defeat in life. He feels halted in his progress toward his desired and expected goal. He has a profound feeling of dissatisfaction with life and with his degree of success in it. He manifests a belligerent type of psychological activity, directed toward a goal of personal superiority. To compensate for his impending defeat, he develops an attitude of criticism and hostility toward others who are made responsible for his own lack of success. He has as a guiding line the idea that he must always be given special consideration, and tends to picture himself as the center of his surroundings. These attitudes are "prepared early in childhood, tested, blunted and protected against the most serious objections of reality" (5, p. 255). Every outbreak of paranoia occurs when the patient finds himself in a dangerous situation where he perceives that the place in life he seeks is definitely lost. "This happens as a rule on the eve of some undertaking, the coming on of old age" (5, p. 258). This is what Dreikurs has called a "crisis situation" (9). According to Adler:

> Psychosis may be regarded as the intellectual suicide of an individual who feels himself unequal to the demands of society or the attainment of his own goal. In his backward movement there is discoverable a secret *actio in distans,* a hostility toward reality. . . . The self-evaluation of the paranoic [in line with his active, self-centered striving for universal superiority] is intensified to the point of similarity to the deity . . . [This compensation] shows its weakness in its speedy renunciation . . . of the demands of society, . . . the transference of the field of action to the domain of the non-real. . . . The patient clearly lacks faith in himself, and his mistrust and unbelief . . . force him toward the construction of cosmogenic and religious ideas. . . . These ideas of the paranoiac are very hard to correct because the patient needs them just in this particular form if he is to establish his point of view. . . . They permit him . . . to adhere to his fiction of superiority without putting it to the test, for he can always ascribe the blame [for his failure] to the hostility of others (5, pp. 257-258).

Masculine protest. Adler's objections to the libido theory, used by Freud to explain paranoid schizophrenia, included three major points (3): (a) Libido is not the motive force behind mental illness; instead, the patient is motivated by the "final goal" he has chosen. (b) Sexual impulses do not cause illness. The sexual symptoms in the mentally ill originate in the imaginary antithesis between "masculine" and "feminine." Their sexual behavior in life and fantasy follows the direction of the imaginary goal of enhanced masculinity, the "masculine protest," in men as well as women. The picture of the sexual neurosis—which would include Schreber's delusions—is "nothing more than a portrait depicting the distance which the patient is removed from the imaginary goal of masculinity and the manner in which he seeks to bridge it" (3, p. x). The sexual symptoms are therefore a "jargon," a *modus dicendi.* (c) The assumption that the patient is under the control of infantile wishes is an error. "In reality, these infantile wishes stand under the compulsion of the imaginary goal" (3, p. x).

Adler's concept of masculine protest is often misunderstood. It embodies the neurotic's "wish to be a complete man," and should be seen in connection with one of the fundamental hypotheses of Adlerian theory (6) which has its roots in biology. The hypothesis states that all life tends to move from "low" to "high," all living beings attempt to compensate for defects which have low survival value, and that man tries to compensate also for subjectively perceived defects, realistic or not (the feeling of inferiority), by trying to attain a compensatory and equally subjectively perceived position of strength or security.

The masculine protest includes the patient's idea that if he were a "real man" he would no longer be inferior or defective or at a disadvantage in life. If he makes being a "real man" (according to his private conception) his goal in life, he overvalues masculinity and its symbols, and tends to rebel against anything which, he fancies, makes him less masculine. Since this kind of goal corresponds to one of absolute superiority, the patient never succeeds in finding a satisfactory integration among his fellows. Therefore, the patient's quest for strength, security and significance is doomed to failure, and he never overcomes his inner feeling that he is inferior, no matter how much he deludes himself to the contrary.

Adler considered the particular form of striving for superiority which is expressed in the masculine protest to be a cultural phenomenon, resulting from the unequal position of the sexes in our society, with the higher value assigned to masculinity (4, p. 21).

The secondary, increased masculine protest. As early as 1910 Adler (1) pointed out that men as well as women have the capacity to be submissive as well as aggressive and that the former is frequently taken as being "feminine," the latter as being "masculine." When in a child and later in the adult there is uncertainty as to his sexual role, and the individual tends toward neurosis, "the natural uncertainty, the vacillation and doubt, become fixed and reinforcements are carried to both poles of the hermaphrodite nature" (4, p. 22). This is "psychological hermaphroditism."

> Psychological hermaphrodites tend sometimes in the feminine and sometimes in the masculine direction. Along with this they will make efforts toward self-consistency . . . This usually initiates a compromise: feminine behavior in men (e.g. shyness and submission, masochism, homosexuality, etc.), masculine role

146

in women (emancipation tendencies, polyandry, compulsion neurosis as disturbance of the feminine role, etc.). Or one finds an apparently random co-existence of masculine and feminine character traits (1, p. 76; 7, p. 47.) The neurosis breaks out when the masculine protest has failed in a main line. The feminine traits then apparently predominate, but only under continuous increase of the masculine protest and pathological attempts to break through along masculine side lines. The outcome of such attempts differs. Either they succeed without bringing real satisfaction and harmony, or they fail likewise, as often in neurosis, and force the patient further into the feminine role, into apathy, anxiety, and mental, physical and sexual insufficiency, etc.—which are further on exploited as means toward power (1, p. 79; 7, p. 50).

This phenomenon of striving for masculine power through feminine means is what Adler called the "secondary, increased masculine protest through detours" (1, p. 80). It is understood as "the occasion for all perversions" (4, p. 22), including homosexuality, and may be found in all mental disorders, including paranoia (1, p. 77).[3]

The function of hallucinations. Regarding the phenomenon of hallucinations found in schizophrenia Adler stated:

> This quality [the ability to hallucinate] is more clearly apparent and more easily discerned in childhood than afterwards. We [adults] are compelled either greatly to limit or even completely to exclude hallucination as such because of its contradiction with rational thinking . . . Only in those cases where the self has separated itself from the community and approximates a condition of isolation, are the clamps removed (2, p. 53). We regard the hallucination as the expression of a personality when in a peculiar position (2, p. 54).

"Both hallucinations and dreams . . . prove to be contrivances for objectifying those subjective impulses to whose apparent objectivity the patient unconditionally surrenders himself" (5, p. 259), allowing himself to move in his chosen direction without feeling responsible for such action.

----

3 Freud, in his analysis of the Schreber case, mentions Adler's 1910 paper, stating that at one point Schreber manifests "a true masculine protest, to use Adler's expression" (11, p. 426), but otherwise briefly dismisses the paper.—Ed. note.

Sullivan's Theory of Schizophrenia and Paranoia

The work of Harry Stack Sullivan, though independently conceived, in many respects is strikingly similar to the views of Adler, and advances, expands and adds to these views. According to Sullivan: "The paranoid dynamism is rooted in (1) an awareness of inferiority of some kind, which then necessitates (2) a transfer of blame onto others" (19, p. 54).

Sullivan, like Adler, dismisses the contention that repressed homosexuality causes paranoia, and explains, instead, that such a patient cannot face the idea of being intimate with anyone (19, p. 157). The frequent concern with homosexuality in such patients is ascribed to incomplete development of the personality in the preadolescent and adolescent phases (19, p. 150).

Sullivan says that the essence of the schizophrenic state is the failure of the self-system (a concept similar to Adler's life style) to reserve attention to the types of referential processes that can be consensually validated. Sullivan and Adler both consider "private sense" or "private logic" as key concepts. The psychotic operates according to a personal logical system which does not have "consensual meaning." In Adler's words, it does not make "common sense." It is, nevertheless, a system that the psychotic considers valid and which he constructs in such a way that reality is effectively disposed of and cannot interfere with the private logic.

"What we discover in the self-system of a person undergoing schizophrenic change is then, in its simplest form, an extremely fear-marked puzzlement . . . [using] rather generalized and anything but exquisitely refined referential processes in an attempt to cope with what is essentially a failure at being human—a failure at being anything that one could respect as worth being" (19, pp. 184-185). Thus Sullivan stresses, even more than Adler does, the extreme feeling of inferiority from which the schizophrenic suffers.

When he discusses the paranoid attitude, Sullivan says: "Here the paranoid dynamism—the transfer of blame has come into being through shifting the mythological and diffusely focused thinking in the direction of one's being the apotheosis of all that one has wished to be" (19, p. 337). Thus, Sullivan also considers that the private goal of superiority is the key factor in paranoia.

One difference from Adler is that Sullivan uses the psychoanalytic concept of regression although without the ideas of fixation at developmental stages, whereas Adler speaks about "backward movement." For Sullivan the psychotic moves back to the private mental state of infancy. Adler is less concerned with the backward movement in *time,* but focuses on the social *distance* that the patient generates between himself and others;

thus, "backward movement" is social withdrawal into a state where reality is discarded.

Adlerian Interpretation of the Schreber Case[4]

Adler seems to have mentioned the Schreber case only once (3, pp. 261-262), while describing the masculine protest: "The antithesis masculine-feminine was the important factor" in the development of Schreber's illness (3, p. 262).

> An Adlerian interpretation of the case unfortunately suffers from the fact that, although Schreber did write about his family, this important information was at the time not acceptable for publication in the *Memoirs*, and is now lost. Nor do the *Memoirs* contain a single early recollection. Thus, the familiar material used by Adlerians to arrive at an understanding of a person, the family constellation and early recollections, are unavailable. Only the symptoms, the content of the delusions and hallucinations, an account of the course of the illness, and the report of Dr. Weber to the court are available.

Exalted goal. Throughout the *Memoirs* one finds hints, implications and sometimes definite statements which illumine Schreber's underlying values and his attitudes toward life. He evaluates himself highly, "a human being of high intellect, of uncommon keenness of understanding and acute powers of observation" (p. 62). His high standards are indicated when he stresses that on becoming *Senats-praesident* he wanted to do his job with "unquestionable efficiency" (p. 63). Since he states that the other judges with him were older and he felt he had to show his worth, one surmises that he needed an unquestionably superior position to be content and that in his moment of greatest success he most questioned his ability to succeed as he wished. Throughout, Schreber defends his own prestige and esteem, excuses all his behavior, rises—through his delusional reasoning—to a position superior to all, even to God. God is seen as the powerful creator who, out of ignorance, goes contrary to the "order of the world" (p. 75), but Schreber wins out over this powerful antagonist and

---

[4] In this section, page numbers without a reference number refer to the *Memoirs* (18).

competitor by reason of his superior intellect and natural morality.

Schreber frequently mentions his superior morality and his interest in order. "Few people have been brought up according to such strict moral principles as I, and throughout life practiced such moderation especially in matters of sex, as I venture to claim for myself" (p. 208). He pictures himself as the only person who knows the truth, and in his over-valuation of the importance of knowing everything, he explains every event he observes in his own terms. "Order" is an important value. He prefers it to be *his* order; an order in which he is moral, pure, all-knowing; an "order of the world" which is more sublime than anyone else's (p. 54). He "proves" over and over again that he is "right," "truthful," "moral" and otherwise superior.

Masculine protest. Schreber who must have always doubted his masculinity was much concerned with the question of superiority-inferiority, expressed in the antithesis masculine-feminine. He refers to the higher value of masculinity, and his own worth as expressed in his masculinity. He describes the "male state of blessedness" (p. 52) as superior to the female state. During the early part of his illness, he tried to "act like a man," but the "voices" decried his lack of manliness (p. 108).

For Schreber, being "unmanned" (p. 99) was equated with "killing me" and "destroying my reason." "Unmanning" equalled "allowing my body to be prostituted like that of a female harlot." At the same time, all his nerves were pure and his purpose holy; therefore he was safe from permanent harm. He feared for "my life, my manliness, my reason" (p. 114). "I suppressed every feminine impulse," "timidity" and "feminine anxiety" (p. 129). Any indication of weakness whatever Schreber assigned to the female gender. All this accords with the concept of masculine protest.

Secondary masculine protest (psychological hermaphroditism). At a certain point Schreber decided he could better achieve his superior goal by being the female Redeemer of mankind rather than by continuing to "protest" his maleness. "Every other aim of manly ambition, and every other use of my intellectual powers in the service of mankind, is now all closed to me" (p. 149). It is, therefore, logical to behave like a woman. He thus took on the feminine role, which he then exploited as a means toward his goal of exalted superiority. He almost states in his own words the dynamics of this arrangement when he writes: "I would like to meet the man who faced with the choice of either becoming a demented human being in male habitus or a spirited female, would not perfer the latter" (p. 149).

The "order of the world" *requires* Schreber to experience the "voluptuous" sensations of a female having intercourse (p. 208). Thus he defends the integrity of his sexual morality while better playing the role of a woman (a person who in his eyes is naturally voluptuous, less moral and of lower intellect). The concept of "unmanning" is central to the development of his case. He first mentions a dream, or fantasy while half asleep, that it would be nice to be a woman having intercourse (p. 63). This foreshadowed the first illness. In the second illness he developed the delusion that his doctor and attendants were conspiring to turn him into a woman and abuse him sexually. Later it was God who wanted to "unman" him by means of divine rays and by first destroying his reason.

Schreber now becomes God's protagonist (Fleschig having long since been relegated to an unimportant position). He assumes that he is the only living human left since the world was partially destroyed in the titanic struggle between himself and God. In his delusions of grandeur he thus allocates himself a supreme role in which only God is worthy to be his opponent. Schreber found a reconciliation in the idea that he was a Redeemer who had to allow himself to be transformed into a female in order to carry out his mission.

He discovered that he can avoid the necessity of playing the male role by "proving" that God is transforming him into a woman and that this is a beneficial act for the whole universe because he will give birth to a new race of humans to repopulate the world. In this way Schreber can now be a person of even greater worth *by not being masculine*. He is even more important than God, because the latter now has to depend on Schreber to repopulate the world. Thus in one stroke he established his divinity and excused himself from his perceived responsibilities of masculinity at the same time.

This is the point at which Schreber "broke down," the so-called "schizophrenic break" or the "fragmentation of the ego," the withdrawal from reality. It is at this point that the patient decides to disregard reality. The rest is attempts at restitution in line with his private logic.

Theme of the delusions. Here the author will develop a point, consistent with Adlerian theory, that the chief content of the schizophrenic's delusions and/or hallucinations shows the crucial mistake in his life style. The delusions point to the "imperative" goal that he believes is absolutely necessary to his worth as a human being; its lack would make him irrevocably inferior to his fellow men. For this imagined lack he constantly and unsuccessfully tries to compensate or cover up. The attainment of this superiority is the fixed goal he constantly pursues. Thus, if one patient's delusions center around money and wealth, we would expect that in his past life he always considered wealth or affluence a necessity without which he could not feel worthwhile. Another patient's delusions may be primarily religious, and we would expect a deep, underlying concern with problems such as morality, eternal life, etc., depending on the particular religious training and conviction of the patient. The rule would be: What is most highly valued by the patient as making him worthwhile and having a place of significance among his fellows (whether it be masculinity, power, godliness, etc.) becomes in his delusions of persecution, what his persecutors try to destroy and what he usurps to himself in his delusions of grandeur.

The important issue for Schreber is his personal value which he equates with masculinity, intellect and morality. It is these which he fears he will lose; which he assumes his enemies are trying to destroy.

Having found his solution in slowly becoming a female in order to give birth to a new race of beings, this being the "true order of the world," Schreber now relates that he *has to work at being female* "in order to *prevent* the withdrawal of those divine rays" that are effecting the sexual transformation. If he tries to avoid behaving like a woman, his sense of well-being decreases (p. 210).

This passage has been overlooked by other commentators who have apparently only assumed that Schreber was rationalizing and justifying his playing the role of a woman. Actually, it is much more than that. A delusional system needs constant reinforcement or it will dissolve under the impact of reality. This is especially true when enough restitution has occurred so that reality is not completely denied by the patient. From the Adlerian view, any symptom must be continually nurtured in order to maintain its effectiveness in accomplishing its purpose. Each patient finds justification for the existence of his symptoms in his own particular way. Schreber, by play-acting a woman, maintains and reinforces his delusion of being slowly transformed and keeps himself in training for the role he has chosen, just as a martyr type confirms his nobility and self-sacrifice by seeking to expose himself to situations where he can suffer. Whenever any stress occurs, he has one solution: He acts like a woman and he feels better. Even when no stress is apparent he may act like a woman in order to keep himself in training, so to speak, like a conscientious athlete. And yet his deep-down opinion of femininity is again apparent in his choice of cheap trinkets with which he bedecks himself when he acts the woman.

Summary

According to Adlerian theory, Schreber did not at all become psychotic because he had homosexual impulses. He became psychotic because (a) he was isolated from his fellow men, (b) he overvalued the importance of his masculinity, his intellect and his morality, and (c) he felt completely lost when these were threatened when he was in positions of responsibility and faced with perhaps the most severe test of his actual abilities.

The moralistic, righteous, probably sexually inhibited Schreber finds surcease from his unsuccessful struggle to be a significant *male* by being transformed into a female of supreme significance, and justifies his abdication from his previous goal of intellectually and morally superior masculinity by convincing himself that feminine "voluptuousness" is a higher duty to God (18, p. 210).

REFERENCES

1. Adler, A. Der psychische Hermaphroditismus im Leben und in der Neurose (1910). In *Heilen und Bilden*. Munich: Reinhardt, 1914. Pp. 74-83.

2. Adler, A. Contributions to the theory of hallucinations (1912). In *The practice and theory of Individual Psychology*. Paterson, N.J.: Littlefield Adams, 1959. Pp. 51-58.

3. Adler, A. *The neurotic constitution* (1912). New York: Dodd, Mead, 1926.

4. Adler, A. Psychical hermaphrodism and the masculine protest— the cardinal problem of nervous diseases (1912). In *The Practice and Theory of Individual Psychology*. Paterson, N.J.: Littlefield Adams, 1959. Pp. 16-22.

5. Adler, A. Melancholia and paranoia (1914). In *The practice and theory of Individual Psychology*. Paterson, N.J.: Littlefield Adams, 1959. Pp. 246-262.

6. Adler, A. *What life should mean to you* (1931). New York: Putnam Capricorn Books, 1958.

7. Adler, A. *The Individual Psychology of Alfred Adler*. New York: Basic Books, 1956.

8. Adler, K. A. Life style in schizophrenia. *J. Indiv. Psychol.*, 1958, 14, 68-72.

9. Dreikus, R. Personal communication.

10. Federn, P. *Ego psychology and the psychoses*. New York: Basic Books, 1952.

11. Freud, S. Psychoanalytic notes upon an autobiographical account of a case of paranoia (dementia paranoides) (1911). In *Collected papers*. Vol. 3. London: Hogarth, 1925. Pp. 385-470.

12. Grauer, D. Homosexuality in paranoid schizophrenia as revealed by the Rorschach test. *J. consult. Psychol.*, 1954, 18, 459-462.

13. Klein, Henriette R., & Horwitz, W. A. Psychosexual factors in the paranoid phenomena. *Amer. J. Psychiat.*, 1949, 105, 697-701.

14. Knight, R. P. The relationship of latent homosexuality to the mechanism of paranoid delusions. *Bull. Menninger Clin.*, 1940, 4, 149-159.

15. Landis, C. Review of *Memoirs of my nervous illness* by D. P. Schreber. (London: Dawson, 1955.) *Contemp. Psychol.*, 1957, 2, 13.

16. Macalpine, Ida, & Hunter, R. A. Introduction, notes and discussion. In D. P. Schreber, *Memoirs of my nervous illness.* London: Dawson, 1955.

17. Mowrer, O. H. Notes. In Anonymous, A new theory of schizophrenia. *J. abnorm. soc. Psychol.,* 1958, 57, 226-236.

18. Schreber, D. P. *Memoirs of my nervous illness (1903).* London Dawson, 1955.

19. Sullivan, H. S. *Clinical studies in psychiatry.* New York: Norton, 1956.

20. Walters, O. S. A methodological critique of Freud's Schreber analysis. *Psychoanal. Rev.,* 1955, 42, 321-342.

SCHIZOPHRENIA AND SEXUAL BEHAVIOR*

Not too many years ago in psychiatry, the most fashionable theories of causation of mental illness held that functional mental disorders had a sexual etiology. Thus, many neuroses were said to result from oedipal conflicts, paranoia was said to be a defense against homosexuality, and schizophrenic behavior and ideation demonstrated the naked sexuality of the "id" with its pleasure seeking drives unhampered by the censorship of an intact "ego." There is no doubt that sexual disturbance is a prominent part of the schizophrenic picture, but modern theories of etiology lay less stress on sexual impulses and more on the disturbed relationship with the world, of which sex is a part rather than a whole.

In discussing the relationship between sex and schizophrenia, Weiner[1] says: "The patient's sexual life is virtually always disturbed. Either he further shuns all sex relationships or he suddenly engages in excessive promiscuity, never achieving satisfaction. Again, he may demonstrate in his sexual behavior the entire gamut of perverse acts, but generally there is a decline in sexual activity except perhaps of the masturbatory nature."

All Aspects of Life Are Disturbed

But in schizophrenia, the social, emotional, economic, political, and intellectual life is also disturbed. Even physiological functions and basic "survival" behavior are disturbed. Not only is there usually a decline in sexual activity *with others,* but "there is a progressive decline in relationships to and contact with others. . . . "[1]

---

* Reprinted by permission from *Medical Aspects of Human Sexuality,* 1971, 5, 144-153.

More than any other "group" of people, schizophrenics have unsatisfactory transactions with life. Since the schizophrenic is a social misfit, he seldom gets the pleasure and security the rest of us get from friends, lovers, and associates. Sometimes he finds some security within the bosom of his family, but all too often at the price of crippling his image of himself and of accepting a distasteful subservient role. The pleasures he finds with his family are too often of a perverted type. While he may cling to a parent or spouse out of dependency and discouragement, he is apt to punish and distress this same person and take a perverse pleasure in doing so. Such relationships do not lead to improved social intercourse. All in all, in his transactions with life, the schizophrenic is almost never at ease, confident or trusting.[2]

There is no specific sexual disturbance in schizophrenia, because schizophrenia itself is a protean condition manifesting a wide range of behavioral, emotional, and perceptual symptoms. We can examine the symptoms of schizophrenia to select those symptoms that seem sexual in nature, and we can also examine the whole gamut of social relationships and attitudes which are associated with sexual activity in our culture. At all times, it is important to remember that sex is a *challenge* in our society. It is associated with marriage, love, attractiveness, the ability to court and seduce, masculinity, femininity, the ability to perform, the ability to please the partner, and is at the same time a large moral issue. All these issues require that certain types of social relationships be established, and the successful establishment of social relationships is extremely difficult for the schizophrenic who generally has a low self-esteem and who does not expect to solve his social problems by following the methods used by the majority of our society.

Sexual Challenges

Masculinity is a measuring stick by which many young men evaluate themselves. The male who doubts his masculinity, yet overvalues it as a goal, is tormented by feelings of shame and inadequacy. The frequent paranoid concern with homosexuality is actually a concern for *masculine* honor and an attempt to deny inadequacy.

157

Love is another difficult challenge for the schizophrenic. He may desire a close relationship, but is seldom willing to chance it. Partly, he has felt injured in his past close relationships; partly, he does not know how to make a mature loving response. He tends to discourage in himself those emotions that would move him closer to others, because he finds them uncomfortable.

Sexual impulses themselves are often uncomfortable for him because their usual function, to move one toward intimacy, is unacceptable to him. He prefers his seclusive attachment, to remain emotionally indifferent to intimacy. Thus, he may subdue his sexual impulses or turn them into a caricature. He may train himself to expect trouble from sex by creating fantasies of all kinds of dire consequences from sexual activity: that his thoughts are immoral and will damn him, that sexual activity will sap his strength, that his lewd desires make him a wild animal, and so forth. He may react to sexual impulses or feelings of attraction by feeling that he is bewitched, hypnotized, that others exert evil influence over him, etc. Because he prefers his ivory tower of detachment, he avoids flesh and blood relationships. If he cannot maintain the detachment, close proximity to a sexual situation can send him into a "sexual panic" in which he confusedly tries to avoid the proximity and either run away from it or attack and drive away the person who seems to influence him.

One adolescent male permitted an older girl to fondle and kiss him. He remained detached and clinical. He reported that the experience did not arouse him and that he probably would not bother again. Shortly thereafter he began to have homosexual fantasies. The occurrence of the fantasies seemed to show that he *had* been aroused by the experience with the girl. By having homosexual fantasies he was effectively denying that it was the girl (who remained available) that interested him.

One young girl was afraid of marriage itself. She had been engaged three times and each time had developed a psychotic episode which required hospitalization. Naturally, the engagement was terminated. After a few months, she would recover, return to the outside world and resume sexual relationships. She never permitted herself to "fall in love" and had become engaged only because her mother wanted her to marry.

Because sex is an important challenge in our lives, sexual situations are common precipitating incidents of acute psychotic states. The first precipitating incident in schizophrenia is often a sexual one.

One young man was a soldier in the occupation forces in Germany. He had been raised as a good, serious, obedient boy. Comparing himself to his father and brother, he had felt less adequate than they, because he was less bombastic and assertive. His barrack mates were enjoying bachelors' lives with the fraüleins, but he avoided such engagements, partially doubting his maleness and partially feeling morally superior. One day a male officer tried to seduce him. He refused and became terrified. Frightened of the officer, he began to anticipate some dreadful revenge against himself. Within a week, he was hallucinating, posturing, and agitatedly denying that he had done wrong. He could not cope with the conflict between his picture of masculinity, his feeling of inadequacy, the necessity to take a stand against the potential seducer, and his usual role of being a good little boy.

A 24-year-old European girl was descended from aristocratic stock. She had been trained to think of herself as superior and especially worthy. The move to America, the death of her idealized father in the war, the subsequent death of her mother, and the necessity to support herself by office work endangered her self-esteem, but she managed to preserve her high opinion of herself by thinking that she was a beautiful virginal girl who would meet a man like her father and be appreciated and loved by him. She was always ready for such an encounter: immaculately groomed, very nicely dressed, and ready to become angry at any casual sexual comment by a man. She had friends, male and female, enjoyed dances and dated frequently without serious interest. One day she met a compatriot who looked like her father. He was pleasant, courteous and attentive, and she was charmed. He dated her and kissed her and she became aroused. After several dates, he spoke casually of marriage and told her that he could recognize that she was in love with him. He then mysteriously stopped calling and dating her. She was much too proud to call him or even to inquire about him among their circle of friends. She saw him once at a party. He noticed her but did not come to speak to her. She felt crushed and betrayed. Her dream was dashed just as it appeared to be reaching fruition.

She became obsessed with thoughts of the man, depressed, unable to work or to enjoy anything. She fancied she saw the man's face in the crowd, in the street, and at movie shows, and she stayed home to avoid such distressing moments. She evolved the theory that she was under a hypnotic spell cast by the man and that his intentions toward her had been purely malevolent. After two months she made an unsuccessful suicide attempt with drugs and was hospitalized. Her chief way of maintaining her self-esteem had been destroyed. She felt that everyone knew about her humiliation and that she could never face her friends again.

Marriage itself is a troublesome issue for the schizophrenic (as seen in the preceding example). It can seem such a fateful step that it becomes too hard or too dangerous to decide when, whom, and under what circumstances to marry. It is the rigid high-flown goal of the schizophrenic which again creates an obstacle here. The rest of us fall in love and follow our feelings, tempered with a modicum of common sense. The schizophrenic cannot so easily take a chance. The idea that we may be making a wrong choice is frightening enough to all of us as we contemplate the many years we expect to spend with a mate. It is much more frightening to the person who anticipates trouble in closeness, dreads intimacy, fears exposure of his weaknesses and assumes that he is unlovable. It is sometimes a lot safer to think that one is homosexual. It becomes such a wonderful excuse for avoiding the challenge of marriage.

The schizophrenic sometimes has as his goal a refusal to submit to logic of living. Falling in love would mean that the other person has gained some power over him. He desires to keep himself above such relationships and thus retain his freedom from submission. It becomes a matter of pride to him to be able to control his feelings. If he also feels "un-lovable," then he dares not permit himself tender affections except at a safe distance. It is much safer to fall in love with a Hollywood star, a television personality, or a disembodied voice over the radio. Letters can even be written to these people.

Sex, marriage, falling in love, even ordinary courting challenges us to risk our self-esteem by valuing the attention of another. The schizoid's self-esteem is built upon flimsy premises and he usually does not dare to openly expose himself to the judgment of his peers. If, under this handicap, he decides to seek sexual contacts, he must do it under safe-guards that protect him from failure.

Brief, fleeting relationships are not restricted to the schizoid but in him they are often his only relationships. An example of such relationships is described in a recent popular song, "Gentle on My Mind," in which the singer describes how the absolute lack of demands by the sex partner permits him to keep his "sleeping bag rolled up behind your couch" and keeps the partner's image in his mind as he wanders where he pleases. A situation which asks little or no respon-sibility is the favored one for such a person. Like a man away at a convention who wants to stray off the range in search of sexual adventure, he prefers anonymity and wants to avoid sticky situations (although his ineptness may bring them about).

One man moved from city to city and job to job, main-taining a quasi-itinerant status. Being young and attractive he usually found a girl who would fall in love with him and share his quarters. When the girl began pressing for marriage he became restless and dissatisfied and moved on again. This same man maintained a tenuous relationship with his father in another city. He visited the father occasionally, but never stayed more than a few days. In his own thoughts, "home" was where his father was.

The schizoid male often marries, but it is common to find that the marriage occurs because the female did the pursuing. Many such men appeal to the "maternal instinct" in the female, but also many of the females are themselves of disturbed immature character, unable to make a sound judgment about their mates, and harboring unrealistic expectations in the marriage. I recall three such marriages distinctly. In each case an emotionally unstable girl with poor social adjustment was attracted to and pursued a schizoid male who seemed gentle, considerate, nonagressive, and "strong." These girls mistook schizoid reserve and aloofness for strength. They were all disappointed after marriage when their husbands showed neither marital responsibility nor affection. The males, themselves painfully awkward in social relationships, had been flattered by the girls' attentions and not recognizing the latent demands had gone into marriage without much forethought, in the hope that it would give them a feeling of worth and masculinity. When the wife's demands began, the husband's opposition appeared. All three marriages ended in divorce, all parties becoming vastly dissatisfied.

The schizoid female, on the other hand, may marry because she is sought by a male. Often she is escaping into marriage from an unhappy home. How her marriage turns out is basically dependent on how well her husband is willing to assume responsibility.

Another form of safeguarding relationships is promiscuity itself. Indiscriminate sexual contact with many people is a way of finding sexual pleasure which prevents a close relationship with any one person and avoids deeper emotional entanglements. A special characteristic of this promiscuity is its inappropriateness and social gaucherie.

One young girl attached herself to a group of high school students who spent their evenings in a bowling alley. They all abused her sexually until they tired of her and chased her away. She would telephone fraternity houses at a neighboring college and ask for dates. Finally, one of the fraternity houses phoned the police and this temporarily ended her adventures.

In Leonard Bernstein's musical, *West Side Story*, the character "Anybody" represents such a schizoid girl: available but not particularly wanted, anxious to please but not knowing how, feeling rejected but not really knowing how to conform to the group mores for females.

Promiscuity leads sometimes to prostitution and the schizoid girl may become a prostitute. She is highly unlikely to be successful at her calling, however, and her life leads in the direction of increasing depravity and despair.

One such girl was married to a taxicab driver who acted as a procurer for her. She and her husband separated after a few years and she went into business for herself. A tavern owner was sympathetic and permitted her to solicit in his tavern. She maintained a regular clientele for a few years but was never aggressive enough to do well and she became increasingly autistic and withdrawn.

Bizarre Sexual Behavior in the Schizophrenic

Avoidance and gauche behavior are not limited to the schizophrenic, and they can be found in almost any adolescent struggling with the problems of sexual and social adaptation. Many young people make unfortunate marriages, and promiscuity occurs for many reasons. There are, however, certain kinds of sexual behavior which are symptoms of a psychotic state. This kind of sexual behavior is rarely found in the nonpsychotic person, and when we see it we are justified in presuming that the symptom represents psychotic pathology.

The common psychotic symptoms which include aberrant or inappropriate sexual behavior are:

1. *Comical attempts at seduction.* A psychotic patient may try to show that he is attracted to someone by displaying his genitals, trying to touch or feel the other person, or by making inappropriate sexual comments.

2. *Displays of hostility.* The psychotic patient cannot always deal well with his sexual feelings. A patient attracted to a young student nurse may be quite uncomfortable with his feelings. He may try to resolve the problem by physically attacking the nurse as if she were the cause of his discomfort.

In his attempts to keep the social world at a distance, the schizophrenic sometimes engages in deliberately shocking behavior. The best way to shock others is to violate the cherished taboos of the others. Thus, the schizophrenic may use foul vituperative language, smear feces, try to urinate on the other, make lewd comments, and otherwise drive away the bothersome people by annoying or embarrassing them to the point where they will avoid him.

But distance-keeping is not always his only object. He generally feels so inferior and handicapped in his relation to others that, like a spiteful child he may enjoy a feeling of power from his ability to make others angry and uncomfortable. For this purpose, sexual comments and annoying sexual behavior have value because of their power to force others to notice. Sometimes it is the only feeling of self-esteem the abject patient can achieve, like a prisoner hurling insults at his captors and refusing to cooperate with them.

3. *Impulsive sexual behavior.* A psychotic is someone who has discarded common sense and uses a private sense of his own. He may not feel obliged to follow the rules of behavior the rest of us use, and therefore can permit himself to make and follow his own rules. Thus, he feels free to parade in the nude if he wishes, to masturbate when he pleases, and otherwise to give in to his impulses. Bizarre, regressed sexual behavior is far less common today than it was before the advent of the phenothiazines. However, during acute psychotic states, sexual posturing, open masturbation, and other exhibitionistic behavior can still be seen.

4. *Autistic fantasies and delusions.* One can find the most elaborate sexual fantasies in the schizophrenic. These fantasies often center around a person who is only slightly known by the schizophrenic or known only as a public image. Favorite objects of fantasies are radio and television personalities.

One girl spent the day in her bedroom listening to her radio. She claimed that one announcer was in love with her and was sending her secret messages. She spent her time decoding the secret meaning of his announcements. She wanted to be ready for the time he would send her a message to come to him.

A man fell in love with a television singer and felt that she reciprocated his feelings. He sent her a postcard proposing marriage, then become acutely upset, delusional and hallucinating. He was afraid she would immediately seek him out and accept his proposal, and he wanted to run away and hide.

Another woman went even further. She wrote and visited the television personality with whom she was having a fantasied love affair. She was treated cordially by the entertainer (who was always careful to see her only in public) and was even introduced to his wife. She nevertheless maintained that they would be united in the future after the entertainer had completed his current commitments.

On first examination, the presenting signs of schizophrenia may be vague or bizarre complaints in any part of the body, or delusional complaints often accompanied by ideas of reference. Some of these delusions and somatic complaints are referable to sex.

One young theology student had been under considerable moral stress as he tried to achieve moral perfection. He was admitted to a hospital with an acute paranoid psychosis. He was able to report that the first symptom he experienced was an auditory hallucination in which he heard voices accusing him of improper sexual thoughts.

Another patient reported that the first time he knew something was wrong was when he noticed people looking at him queerly and talking about him. He concluded that the people must be thinking he was homosexual.

A woman reported that a man who was interested in her was entering her room while she was asleep, drugging her, and having intercourse with her.

Another woman complained of severe vaginal pruritus. Examination revealed only irritation from excessive scratching. Psychological testing showed a schizophrenic process.

Fantasies of pregnancy are a common symptom in female schizophrenics and have even been found in male patients.

5. *Sexual offenses by the schizophrenic.* I can no longer count the number of schizophrenics I have examined, yet the number of sex offenders I have seen is perhaps a few dozen. I cannot recall any schizophrenic who was a chronic sex offender. It is true that a schizophrenic may get himself arrested for exhibiting, but the true exhibitor is not schizophrenic. I assume a schizophrenic may commit rape, but I

have never seen it. I consider schizophrenics rather innocuous people who are subject to anger just like anyone else, but not at all likely to commit sexual crimes. Of course some schizophrenics are bullies, but many more are victims.

There is no particular indication that the sexual perversions are found more frequently in schizophrenia than in the population at large. The schizophrenic may often consider himself perverted and use this as further evidence that he is a loathsome and unlovable person. This reinforces his desire to keep distance from others. He can even convince himself that he doesn't deserve to be in the company of others.

One man was obsessed by sexual thoughts, especially thoughts of masturbating. He spent the day trying to fight off the "dirty thoughts." He would spend hours in the shower if allowed, until his skin was macerated. He walked with his arms held away from his body, afraid he would touch himself.

Summary

Since schizophrenia can produce such a broad disturbance of human behavior, it is not surprising to find sexual disturbance as well. The sexual disturbances are of two categories: (1) They are the consequences of severely distorted interpersonal relationships, which prevent the schizophrenic from pursuing the common sexual goals and using the common social methods for such pursuit. Instead, he avoids, in one way or another, those situations and methods of behavior that would lead to satisfactory sexual relationships with others. (2) They are symptoms of an acute psychotic state with its attendant confusion, disregard of social rules, impulsive behavior, hostility, and autistic preoccupations.

Sexual challenges can precipitate the initial and subsequent schizophrenic episodes, but difficulties in peer relations, in academic or occupational situations, religious questions, and domestic strife are equally common as precipitants.

In general, the schizophrenic is far less sexually active than the rest of the population and gets less satisfaction out of such activity. Just as he gives up in other areas, he eventually abdicates his sexual role, withdrawing where he can from the temptations of life that seem to him to promise only torment. Eventually, he is likely to decide that sex, like the rest of life, is a cheat, a fraud. It may be for others, but not for him. Or perhaps it is only a vast game arranged to perplex and confuse him, and he alternates between suffering the agonies of a failure and a victim, or decides to treat the whole thing as a bad joke not yet discovered by the other humans.

REFERENCES

1. Weiner, H.: Diagnosis and symptomatology; in Bellak, L. (ed.): Schizophrenia: a Review of the Syndrome (New York: Logos Press, 1958), p. 112.

2. Shulman, B. H.: Essays in Schizophrenia (Baltimore: Williams & Wilkins, 1968), p. 55.

SEX FOR DOMINATION *

To be in love is to allow another some power over oneself. It requires trust in human relationships and the courage to face the possibility of hurt

The prominent American psychologist Abraham Maslow conducted a series of experiments and observations in the 1930's on monkeys and apes. In discussing their social behavior he found that in every cage of monkeys at a zoo a dominant overlord was found without exception. This dominant overlord did all the sexual mounting that was observed. In addition, females could be dominant as well as males. A dominant female mounted both males and females in her cage. The subordinate animal mounted very rarely, generally playing the female role in sexual behavior. If there are two drives that lead to sexual behavior—the true sexual drive and the dominance drive—then the dominance drive is prepotent[1]

Maslow expressed his conclusions in the language of the 1930's. We would be less inclined to speak today about the relative power of a drive, since we recognize that personality is a unified whole and that drives are modified to suit the psychic requirements of any particular individual. Maslow's study, however, is an important corroboration of something discussed in a previous paper in *Human Sexuality*,[2] i.e., sexual behavior often occurs for a great number of nonsexual reasons. The behavior looks like sex, sounds like it, feels like it, smells like it, but it is something else. One such very important "something else" is *dominance,* a state of dominating, controlling, or influencing, which is as important to men as it is to monkeys.

The desire for dominance is probably related to the basis of animal life itself. Dominance over the environment is one

---

* Reprinted by permission from *Medical Aspects of Human Sexuality*, 1971, 5, 28-32.

theme of man's history on this planet. Dominance over himself is part of many of his cultures, and dominance over his fellow men is a neurotic and frequently destructive tendency in himself. There are many ways and many areas in which man can strive for dominance. Sex is but one of them. The sexual act is, however, a social function which requires a large measure of human cooperation. It is hedged around with taboos, and it makes a demand for degrees of intimacy uncomfortable to many. However, it is important enough so that very few humans can simply take it or leave it. In such a complex area, all the factors involved in human relationships can often be found in full regalia and sex becomes an arena in which many desires and strivings interpose and influence sexual behavior itself.

Maslow spoke of a sexual drive and a dominance drive. Let us discard his language and rather see behavior as purposive. We can then say that his monkeys used sexual behavior as an expression of the desire for dominance; that is, they used sexual behavior in order to dominate. Various parameters and degrees of domination can be achieved through sexual behavior.

One type of domination is simply the desire to win out over an opponent or situation. If the sexual act is viewed as competitive, then one's will must be imposed upon the sexual transaction. If one partner is willing to submit he can have a type of cooperative sexual relationship with the one who wants his own way; but if both want their own way there will be no sexual transaction at all or a series of tragicomic compromises. Thus, the ardent swain tries to seduce his love to have his will; his love tries to avoid being seduced and permits it only if it is a better way of gaining the upper hand than refusal. A husband feels entitled to his pleasure with his wife whenever he pleases; she refuses to drop everything else to attend to him and makes him wait until she is good and ready.

One couple had a special problem. The wife was sexually aroused at bedtime but the husband was then too sleepy to perform. In the morning the husband was alert and interested, but the wife was still tired and sleepy and would not respond. Since both professed great interest in finding a solution it was recommended that they set the alarm clock for 3 a.m. Each felt the other would be making an equal sacrifice and they agreed with happy results. After a few such sessions, they felt enough good will for each other to perform either in the night or the morning.

Sometimes, sexual behavior demonstrates a concern for not being dominated or for not losing the contest. Thus, not giving in to the other person keeps oneself from losing and the other from winning. Some sexual symptoms demonstrate this principle. Some women are frigid and unresponsive specifically because they do not want to give in. In the male, penile impotence is often a passive covert way of defeating the wife's demands. Premature ejaculation can mean the same thing.

Another parameter of dominance is the desire to manipulate the other person. It is not simply for the purpose of having one's own way, but also includes the goal of making the other submit, of being the "boss." In some pornographic stories the plot calls for the male protagonist to so arouse the female that once she has tasted the ecstasy of sexual surrender she becomes the willing slave and accomplice of her seducer. Sometimes a wife may use sex as a way of rewarding her husband for "good behavior" and punishing him for "bad behavior" for the purpose of trying to control his behavior. The woman who demands gifts as a reward for surrendering may also be interested mainly in exploiting her partner.

The psychotic general in *Doctor Strangelove* did not want any woman to obtain his sexual discharges since he claimed he would be giving part of his "life forces" up to her if she retained his seminal fluid. This is similar to the idea that one can control another if one can stimulate one's partner to orgasm. The male sometimes thinks in terms of "forcing" the female to have an orgasm specifically because he enjoys seeing the woman seemingly lose control of herself. He enjoys "making" her respond to his caresses. The female, of course, can also play this game.

Some people use dominance over another as a way of enhancing the self. Thus, one has more self-esteem if one can dominate another. There are some sexual games that such people play. A common one is connected with oral intercourse. One partner hesitates to take the active role because he views it as putting him in the "inferior" position and relishes the passive role because he feels it elevates him over the other. Some homosexual relationships carry an exaggerated concern with this type of dominance. (One homosexual reported that his main thrill came from seducing another male into undressing and agreeing to intercourse. Whether or not intercourse actually took place was of less concern to him.)

In our society, the concern of the male with his masculine superiority in the sexual area leads to some sad and some comic consequences.

One man used to complain that his wife was less ardent than he and did not completely fulfill her connubial duties. He brought his wife for marriage counseling. The wife pointed out that it was the male's role to be the aggressor and the female's role to be the passive recipient, but also that she did not find herself that interested in sex. In none of her other relationships with her husband was she as non-aggressive as in the sexual area. She was persuaded by the counselor to assert herself more in this area, and when she began to do so she enjoyed sex more. However, she began to complain that her husband was losing his desire and was neglecting her. The husband admitted that he preferred to retain the initiative himself and did not like the idea of his wife making demands upon him. Her assertiveness had gone too far in his estimation; he only wanted her to warm up to him when *he* gave the signal.

Females used to be considered the male's property to be used "at his pleasure." Whether or not the female enjoyed the act was supposedly of no concern (except, perhaps to the unsatisfied wife). Now, however, women are demanding a redefinition of their social role. Their "rights" include, of course, the right to have an orgasm along with the male. Once the male is *forced* to give the woman pleasure he is no longer in the superior position. He is now obligated to perform at a certain level; the female sits in judgment on his performance, winning the dominant position.

The feminists with their beliefs concerning the degradation (putting down) of females as exemplified by the Playboy Bunny are also obviously concerned with the issue of dominance. On a late night talk show a feminist asked Hugh Hefner if he would appear on stage with a puff of cotton on the seat of his pants.

The female, of course, also is concerned with self-enhancement and again may base her feeling of self-enhancement upon her ability to manipulate the male. The woman who knows she is sexually attractive may thus enjoy not only arousing the man she has singled out but also putting him into her service and enjoying his submission to her.

Sadism is a sexual perversion in which the desire to dominate another person can be clearly seen. In De Sade's writings he constantly deals with what is to him the main issue in sex or in life; namely, one person gaining complete control over another. Sex is merely one vehicle for achieving this goal. The sadist is excessively concerned with the issue of personal domination, but it also seems that he must reduce his lover to the status of an object so he can use the object without having to enter into a relationship between equals.

However, when a man pays a prostitute to whip him until he is aroused, who is dominant? When a girl can only achieve orgasm if her partner brutalizes her, which one is dominant? Many sadomasochistic relationships are really cooperative endeavors in which, often, the masochist is the one who calls the tune.

Those who fear that giving in to another means losing control are often afraid to enter into a love relationship. They are afraid of putting themselves in another's hands. "You can't have me, you'll drop me and break me" is their unspoken accusation against all suitable partners.

To be in love is to allow another some power over oneself. It requires trust in human relationships and the courage to face the possibility of hurt and humiliation. Those who feel they can never risk themselves, that they will be used and abused, that they must maintain control of themselves at all times and at all costs, will never feel confortable in love.

Many men continue in a love relationship for a considerable period of time without ever telling the woman that they love her. They act as if saying "I love you" gives the woman some special power. It is as if she could now truly reject the male by denying that she loves him.

If a man's desire to dominate is seen as a drive in itself, then one concludes it is in man's nature to dominate. It is not, however, necessary to see it that way. The person who wants to dominate another is someone who is discouraged about the effectiveness of relationships between equals. He (or she) wants to establish *authority* over the other because he does not trust democratic relationships. He wants to make himself bigger by making the other smaller. He feels threatened if he cannot dominate. The person who can accept himself as an equal of others and can trust the others to accept him does not feel a need to dominate others and believes he will be able to keep others from dominating him. He is more concerned with closeness and friendship than with the balance of power. He does not need power tactics; he can use honesty, sincerity and *caritas* as his trade goods with others.

Karen Horney considered the desire to dominate a cultural phenomenon and a neurotic trait. When a person does not feel fully belonging and does not during his (or her) development experience love, warmth, and other aspects of a healthy child-parent relationship, that child is inclined to a more forceful struggle for attention and seeks an ability to impress others and win them over by some forceful technique. Such children become people who are interested in dominating. From this point of view, Maslow's monkeys were neurotic and the use of sex as a vehicle to dominate another is an indication of imperfect upbringing and mistaken goals.

REFERENCES

1. Maslow, A. H.: Individual psychology and the social behavior of monkeys and apes. Int. J: Indiv. Psychol. 1:4 1935.

2. Shulman, B. H.: Uses and abuses of sex. *Medical Aspects of Human Sexuality* 2:48, Sept. 1968.

GROUP PSYCHOTHERAPY IN A U.S. ARMY POST STOCKADE *

Alfred Adler suggested the use of group treatment techniques for the rehabilitation of offenders:

> While I do not believe it would be possible to give every criminal an individual treatment we could contribute much by a group treatment. I should propose, for instance, that we should have discussions with a great number of criminals on social problems, exactly as we have been considering them here. We should question them and let them answer; we should enlighten their minds and waken them from their life-long dream; we should free them from the intoxication of a private interpretation of the world and so low an opinion of their own possibilities; we should teach them not to limit themselves and diminish their fear of the situations and the social problems which they must meet. I am very sure that we could achieve great results from such group treatment.[1]

It becomes increasingly known that group psychotherapy, in its various forms, is a valuable adjunct to other rehabilitation methods. Indeed, there are opinions that a therapeutic relationship with an asocial or antisocial person is easier to establish and maintain in a group setting, than in an individual setting; because the sociopath's lack of conscience obstructs the rapport between himself and a therapist, but does not obstruct it with a group that he can consider his allies (other sociopaths).

In 1954 the author was in military service as Chief of the Mental Hygiene Consultation Service at Fort Belvoir, Va. The post stockade at this installation is used for short term confinement only. Prisoners with sentences over one year are

---

* Reprinted from *Federal Probation*, March 1957.

1 "The Individual Psychology of Alfred Adler," Heinz L. Ansbacher and Rowena R. Ansbacher, Editors, N.Y., Basic Books, Inc. p. 348.

transferred to disciplinary barracks. Consequently, Fort Belvoir retains mainly the minor offenders in the classifications of petty larceny, military disobedience, and chronic alcoholism in conjunction with violations of military regulations. All of the prisoners are enlisted men who have been tried and convicted by summary or petty court martial.

A psychologically oriented confinement officer at the post stockade had become interested in rehabilitation. He referred a number of cases to the writer for treatment. It soon became obvious that this procedure was not meeting the needs of a great many other prisoners who might welcome treatment. The possibility of utilizing group psychotherapy was discussed and a program was outlined.

The Selection of Patients

The following procedures were used in selecting a group which varied from four to eight patients at any one time. All incoming prisoners were given group tests and were interviewed by a psychologist. The purpose of this initial procedure was to gain an overall view of the problem and to determine which of the prisoners might benefit most from a group approach. The confinement officer was an integral part of the selection procedure and retained the final decision as to which men would enter the program.

The group finally selected were men whose sentences were over three months. All of them were below age 35; one had been in Service fifteen years, the others two years or less. One third of them were slated for undesirable discharges, but with the added provision that this might be revoked at the recommendation of the confinement officer. None of the participants were psychotic and none carried a psychiatric diagnosis of psychoneurosis; however, some showed strong psychoneurotic tendencies chiefly manifested by emotional instability. Most of the group had been classified as passive-aggressive personality; a few were alcoholics. The intelligence range was from low average to superior. Choice of patients was also influenced by the presence of positive factors in the history such as a previously good military record or a strongly expressed desire for help.

Candidates were told that an opportunity was available for them to enter the program; they were informed of its voluntary nature and were told "This is a chance for you to find out why you have gotten into trouble and to learn how to avoid it in the future; it will, also, give you a chance to find out more about yourself and a chance to talk to a psychiatrist. Whatever you say in the group is confidential. The confinement officer and the guards won't know about it. This may be hard for you to believe, but it's true. We plan to trust you and we hope that you'll trust us. You can try it and if you don't like it, you don't have to continue. You'll be excused from other duties to attend. You'll have to make up your own mind about it."

The Therapeutic Setting

Therapists were the author, (a psychiatrist), a psychologist, and a psychology technician, at least two of whom were always present during the sessions. Formalities of military courtesy were dispensed with during the meetings. The therapist remarked, "When I take off my hat here, I am taking off my bars. Forget, if you can, that I am an officer, remember that I am a doctor." Therapists showed by their actions and emotional responses as well as by verbal reassurance that the subject matter was confidential, and that no punishment would follow expression of hostility against the army.

No separate building being available, one corner of the large mess hall was used. Since soldiers were working at the other end, this at first posed a problem of noise, until the group therapy members themselves became interested enough to enforce silence.

The meetings took place once a week for an hour and a half in the afternoon. All participants were excused from their prison duties at this time. An afternoon was chosen that did not conflict with any of the prison rehabilitation programs. No other prisoners and no guards were permitted at the meeting. Participants came voluntarily. They were informed that attendance at the meetings would not influence the prison authorities favorably or unfavorably and that the confinement officer, prison review board and clemency board would continue to judge them by criteria formerly used, such as willingness to work, ability to accept discipline, and evidence of improved attitudes.

The average number of meetings attended by each patient was ten to twelve. Most common cause of termination of attendance was discharge; to duty, to parole status, or to civilian life. Follow-up service was offered and utilized at the offices of the Post Mental Hygiene Consultation Service. Many participants requested individual psychiatric interviews and these were granted. Total duration of the program was six months after which it was terminated because of lack of trained personnel.

The Group Therapy Process

The therapy techniques followed an Adlerian frame of reference. Inherent in this are processes and attitudes which include: (1) understanding the patient in his social setting (2) understanding the private goals toward which he is tending, (3) interpreting the social purpose of the patient's behavior in terms meaningful to the group, (4) treating the patient like a human being with a problem, (5) encouraging him to recognize the existence of the problem, (6) creating cohesiveness in the group by discussion, interaction, and interpreting interaction, (7) clarification, and (8) stressing the idea that people get into trouble because they have become discouraged about their ability to achieve their goals in socially useful ways.

Most frequent topics chosen by the group were sex, and the unfairness of life in the Army, and particularly as represented by the stockade. Actually, the initial choice of topic itself was not so crucial because meaningful interpretations are possible about all topics. Patients were encouraged to understand the meaning of their own and other's behavior. The usual problems of sub-group formation, marginal groups and lack of group feeling in certain patients, arose and were dealt with. Those prisoners who tried to assume a superior attitude were vehemently rejected by the group. The new man who asked, "What do I get out of this?" was condescendingly "told off" with the statement, "I think it's done a lot for me, you just wait and see."

All participants felt that they had gained more knowledge of themselves and others than they had before; indeed, they soon began to talk about the psychological problems of the guards and the possible techniques for avoiding trouble with them. They discussed daily prison occurrences and began to express appreciation for some of the positive aspects of the stockage, whereas, previously they had focused only on what they thought was wrong and unfair. Few prisoners denied their offenses because none of the crimes was of a heinous type. The atmosphere of the group encouraged admission of faults, independent initiative and acceptance of certain realities in life, but discouraged self-abnegation, excessive avowals of repentance and feelings of guilt; according to the concept, "it's what you're going to do, not what you feel, that really counts."

The amount of interest shown by participants was gratifying. Many felt it was the first time they had been treated like adult humans; as their self-esteem grew, they could esteem others more highly. Attempts to exploit others (what some call "dependency needs") were always interpreted as attempts to exploit. There was quick interest by the group in the problems of individual participants. The group cohesiveness carried over to other stockade situations and these prisoners felt quite superior to those who did not have the advantage of a "psychiatric education."

Results

In such a short term project the results are not easy to evaluate. The following criteria were used to measure improvement, (1) the therapists' opinion regarding significant change in the patient's behavior, (2) the confinement officer's opinion regarding improved behavior, (3) the opinion of the commanding officer of the unit to which the patient was sent after discharge. Since some patients were discharged from the Army or transferred off the post, the last criterion was not always available.

As indicated above, the therapists' observations were that the patients changed in the direction of gaining greater insight into the meaning of their own behavior; the patients appeared better able to develop new techniques for relating to authority and peers and generally to develop increased social conformity; this resulted from the decrease in their feelings that everyone was unfair to them. Hostility and bitterness was partially replaced by socially outgoing attitudes and optimism. Their own gain in self-respect was followed by greater respect for others. Not all changed their anti-social behavior, and none of the alcoholics ceased to have a problem with alcohol. Cases receiving the most benefit were those confined for larceny and absence without leave.

Rumors about the program spread through the stockade, among guards and prisoners. Guards at first took a critical attitude; prisoners were condescending, afraid they would be considered "crazy" if they participated in the program. Others tried to exploit it for external advantage, such as parole or discharge from the Army. As the program continued, participants gradually carried back the story that the program offered only help in understanding of self and other humans. This resulted in a more favorable situation for group therapy purposes. Those prisoners who were concerned with personal problems and motivated to examine themselves critically, began to request admission to the program.

A PSYCHODRAMATICALLY ORIENTED ACTION TECHNIQUE IN GROUP PSYCHOTHERAPY *

An important goal in psychotherapy is attainment of insight, which in turn has the tendency to initiate new patterns of thinking and behavior. One method a therapist can use to help the patient attain insight is confrontation: that is, the therapist shows the patient the underlying, real purpose of his behavior and his biased perceptions.

For example, a patient may actually be seeking the noble and desired state of martyrdom through provoking others to abuse him for the private goal of feeling superior to his "tormentors." At the same time the patient will be unaware of his private goal and will believe that he is only pursuing some worthwhile end or that he is an innocent victim. When the patient is confronted with his private goal and helped to see that he actively provokes the abuse himself, his awareness of his behavior pattern helps him try to avoid repeating it and to search, instead, for new ways of behaving.

Method

The method described here is an extension of words into action. Ordinarily, the therapist who understands the patient's goals tries to communicate this information verbally to the patient. The therapist's words are often countered by the patient with other words. If the patient resists accepting the therapist's interpretations, therapy may become a matter of cross-argumentation. In group psychotherapy, a patient may similarly refuse to accept the group's interpretation of his behavior.

The author was conducting a therapy group in which some members continually puzzled and exasperated the others

---

* From *Group Psychotherapy*, Vol. XIII No. 1, J. L. Moreno, M.D., Editor, Beacon House, Inc., Publisher.

by subtly provocative behavior. The latter either withdrew from or became openly antagonistic to the provokers, perceiving them as not fitting into the group and refusing to accept its common purpose. The author considered that a more effective way of helping the provokers attain insight would be to confront them with their motives by letting them experience the group reactions to them in line with their subtle demands. If the members of the group reacted in an exaggerated manner to the patient's neurotic goals, the message might be carried to the patient in a dramatic and forceful way. Instead of only using words, action was employed. This is close to the approach of Moreno.

Action Technique

The group in which this technique was explored had been meeting weekly over a year.* All had been or still were in individual psychotherapy. It contained men and women ranging in age from 20 to 40. None were psychotic.

The plan was discussed during a group session. It was agreed that the group would try to discover the purpose of the irritating and provocative behavior and would then, in an exaggerated way, respond to the behavior, in line with the provocateur's neurotic demands. "If he wants to be a baby, let's treat him like a baby and see if he likes it."

The writer used two independent approaches in the group for determining the faulty goals of the patients: an analysis of early recollections and group discussion of the probable private demands of each patient. One of the patient's goals, an outstanding and obviously faulty one and its chief method of attainment in the group were chosen in order to simplify and dramatize the technique and its effects.

Examples

John, a 26-year-old male, an only child, continually apologized for his behavior, remarks and appearance. He insisted

---

* From *Group Psychotherapy*, Vol. XIII No. 1, J. L. Moreno, M.D., Editor, Beacon House, Inc., Publisher.
Mrs. Adaline Starr was co-therapist of the group.

that he was the most poorly endowed in the group, was stupid, unattractive, unmanly and that he felt inferior to all the others. The group first tried to help him by denying his self-description and pointing out his assets, but had become discouraged and antagonistic toward him.

His early recollection was:

> "I was running alongside a low (unfenced) porch, screaming with fright. My parents, sitting on the porch, saw me run but didn't see anything chasing me. They got up to look and saw that I was being chased by a tiny gosling, so small they couldn't even see its head from where they were sitting."

The patient thus tells us thru his memory that he is absolutely inadequate. He has to run from something so small that no one else would be afraid of it. How can anyone expect him to face adult tasks? He cannot take care of himself, others must protect him and care for him.

The group decided to respond to John as if he actually were inadequate and worthless. They began to ignore him or to deride his remarks. They told him that he couldn't possibly have anything worthwhile to offer but that they suffered his presence because they were too kind to throw him out of the group. A common response when John spoke was, "There you go making stupid remarks again. You are just inadequate, nothing you say is worthwhile," or "if you say it, it must be wrong."

This procedure took place in one group session only. John did not show anger, but refused to talk to anyone after the session was over. He later told the therapist that he was very angry. At the next group session his anger was abated but he spoke of how angry he had been. He seemed surprised that the group accepted his anger. Once he began to apologize and caught himself, saying, "There I go again." The group offered warm feelings and John felt he didn't have to display his inadequacy any longer. Surprisingly, the provocative behavior returned only at long separated intervals, and a simple reminder from another group member was enough for him to catch himself.

George, a 25-year-old male, an only child, verbalized freely in the group. He was willing to discuss his own problems and could engage in badinage with other group members.

He courted the women, was contemptuous of some of the men (whom he considered inferior) and respectful of the other men (to whom he felt inferior) yet competitive with both. His interpretive remarks to other members were generally hostile. The group suspected that behind his outward behavior was an aloofness from the group and a fear of being exposed. He was well-liked by the group because of his charm, but his remarks seemed carefully measured and unspontaneous. The group complained they did not really know him, that he always liked to get the upper hand over them.

His earliest recollection was:

"I was with a young woman, a friend or relative of the family. We were playing. She was lying on the floor and I was sitting on her chest. She was permitting it. It was enjoyable."

The patient needs the willing submission of others to find his place. When others allow him the superior position, he enjoys it and is willing to participate. He wants to be above and supported by others.

The group decided to "Kow-tow" to George. On the day when the session was to be devoted to this, George came late and the others had raised a chair on telephone books so that he could be higher than the others. George entered and smilingly accepted the chair. He was addressed as "Your Highness" and spoken of with adulation. George continued to smile and occasionally gave orders or made requests. He was playing the game. Near the end of the session, he confessed discomfort, saying that he still enjoyed the high position, but didn't like the group finding out he wanted it. He was afraid the group would not "fall" for his charm and intellectual pretences if they knew he wanted to be the center of their admiration. After discussion, George mentioned that he did not really need so much special position since he could be accepted more easily if he were on a level with the others, and that such superiority as he wanted was no true test of his worth anyway. He felt he was not yet ready to give up his goal, but now that everyone knew it, he might try to find his place in the group in more direct and open contest, perhaps by being helpful. He did not need the aloofness any longer. Everyone knew him for what he was and could accept him.

In subsequent group sessions, he continued to be competitive and often hostile but no longer aloof.

Ruth, a 21-year-old female, a middle child, was antagonistic toward patients and therapists alike. Occasionally she "took the floor" to question, criticize or even denounce the behavior of others, including the therapist. Her criticism was often to the point and had a moral quality. The group resented her "holier than thou" attitude. Some members argued with her, called her intolerant and over-critical.

Her earliest recollection was:

> "I was looking out of the second floor window and saw my grandfather coming to the house. He looked like a small old man. He was very shabbily dressed and I didn't like it."

Ruth looks down on others and finds them wanting. Her chief concern with people is to discover their faults, to sit in judgment over them. The group decided to use Ruth as a judge. Each member would make a remark and turn to Ruth asking, "Is that right?" All issues were referred to Ruth for her judgment. She was asked to make critical comments about the deficiencies of each member. Ruth began to catch herself. She was angry after the session but in subsequent sessions, when she offered a comment, she would add, "There I go judging again." She offered her own problems for discussion and said she was more eager to learn than to find fault and fight. She guessed she didn't need to be "righter" or "smarter" than everybody else.

Greta, a 23-year-old female, a first born, who had been dethroned three times (abandoned by father, mother had remarried and left her with grandmother and then mother gave birth to a child who superseded Greta in mother's favor) seemed withdrawn and fearful in the group. She wanted to be liked and appreciated attention, but spoke very little and seemed constantly to expect censure or dislike. The group tried to draw her out, but she pleaded that while she was willing to talk, she didn't know what to say. She claimed she liked everything and everybody in the group, admitted to being afraid of some of the more aggressive people. She had been afraid to enter the group and did so only after months of hesitation. She had been in the group only a few months and did not feel as much a part of it as some of the older members. The group resented what they called her refusal to show her "real feelings."

Her earliest recollections were:

"It was a car accident, I was crossing the street. All I remember is lying on the ground and looking up and seeing the big black shape of a car passing over me . . . "

Greta sees herself as a victim of a danger world. She is "laid low" by life. " . . . I was lying on a cot in the hospital. Grandfather was there. There was an intern in white. Somebody gave me some ice cream and I ate it."

In the midst of suffering, there is ice cream. Perhaps some good can come from getting hurt. " . . . One time I fell and hit my head against the sharp corner of a wall, I was bleeding. I ran home and mother was sorry. She washed the cut and bandaged it. I remember the water in the pan was bloody."

Now her suffering has utility. She can make the mother, who otherwise ignored her, feel sorry for her by getting hurt. She is still impressed by the blood and seems to feel that only suffering has a chance of getting her anywhere. She is an "innocent victim" of life. In suffering there is glory.

The group, in their discussion, expressed much sympathy for Greta and hesitated to "gang up on her." At this point, the therapist suggested they go through with the plan to "help her be a victim and find glory" because the technique had helped others in the group. Greta asserted her willingness to proceed, at which point one member said, "Yes, you're willing to be a victim any time." Greta laughed, as did the others. She then said, "Maybe you don't even have to do it. I feel closer to you all already and I don't think anyone here would want to hurt me." Subsequently in the group meetings Greta spoke more freely, could express likes and dislikes and lost her fearful manner.

Discussion

Being confronted with one's mistaken goals and suddenly realizing them, often leads to an immediate feeling of release of tension and resulting spontaneity of behavior (because the previous defenses are no longer in operation). At the moment when the person catches himself, which is a process of insight and re-evaluation, the goals can change and the defensive distance-keeping operations are, for the moment, at least, suspended.

In addition, while the person's goals may not always change, he may often recognize that he might change them. This thought, though sometimes fleeing, may be the opening wedge into the person's neurotic pessimism. Thirdly, exposure of goals often leads to the patient's recognition that even though the group now knows his weakness, it still will not harm him.

However, it is frequently difficult to "get across" to people, to really make them understand the underlying meaning of their behavior. The most frequently utilized procedure is talking. But people tend to become "therapy deaf," and while they hear and understand concepts, they do not experience them. A much more effective way is to make a person experience the "logical consequences" of his behavior by real-life reactions, such as in the described techniques.

In a therapy group (perhaps in other groups also) the atmosphere is usually one of cooperation and mutual endeavor; therefore, the individual is more ready for insights which would permit him to move "emotionally" closer to the others. This state of "being close" can be described as a feeling of friendliness, mutual acceptance at face value, respect for each other's company. A feeling of belonging or being part of the group or part of a group process is also significant. Conversely, such persons are less inhibited by felt needs, (both resulting from neurotic mistaken assumptions and from cultural pressures) to keep at a distance from each other, compete for prestige, etc. Such a state of mind permits greater spontaneity of behavior, corresponding to greater inner freedom.

It is common knowledge that a stressful experience for a group tends to move its members closer and increases their warmth for each other. In the same way, a stress experience for one member of a group may result in increased acceptance of the individual by the group. Even more so, this greater

186

acceptance is to be expected when the group understands these mistaken motives that lead to irritating behavior, and recognizes that the person has caught himself and reacted in a new way with more warmth to the group. Also each person in the group sees this as a hopeful sign that the group can help its members.

The two immediately demonstrable results are therefore: The changed relationship between the individual and the group, and the stronger feeling of group cohesion.

THE USE OF DRAMATIC CONFRONTATION
IN GROUP PSYCHOTHERAPY *

In a recent paper, a group therapy technique was described which the author found useful in helping certain patients who were subtly provoking other members of the group, achieve insight into their behavior. All of these patients were seen by other group members as antagonistic and, somehow, not accepting the common purpose of the group.

The technique was based upon the hypotheses: (1) that all behavior is goal-directed, (2) that in each person's behavior in the group can be seen his psychic "movement" in relation to the other group members, and (3) that this "movement" reveals the patient's secret intentions, his "private goals." In addition to these hypotheses, it was also postulated that dramatically confronting the patient with the secret, usually unconscious, purpose expressed in his behavior would promote insight by the dramatic uncovering and promote much more rapid acceptance than cross-examination, wise interpretations, reassurance, and logical persuasion.

The essentials of the technique are as follows: The group, perhaps at the instigation of the therapist, discusses the behavior of the patient in question and tries to determine the particular "private goal" of this behavior. This is done by analyzing the behavior itself and by giving the patient a short projective test in the group setting; that is, by asking for the patient's earliest recollections and then analyzing them (Shulman[1]). The group then decides, usually with the patient's consent, to respond to the patient's behavior in an *exaggerated* way *in line with* the patient's neurotic demands. ("If he wants to be a baby, let's treat him like a baby.")

---

* Reprinted by permission from *The Psychiatric Quarterly*, 1962, 36, 93-99.

The technique was so helpful in eliciting constructive change in these patients and promoting a strong group cohesiveness, that the writer tried to find a use for it with all the patients in the group who seemed blocked or slow in making therapeutic progress. In the previous paper, four examples of using the technique were given. Further examples are here presented to clarify further the use of the technique and to present a further explanation of the dynamics involved.

Pamela, a 30-year-old wife and mother, suffering from recurrent depressions, was well liked by the other group members. She was talkative, friendly, and encouraging to others, yet constantly complained that she was not getting well fast enough. Her symptoms interfered with her ability to enjoy her family, though she was always trying to please them. Actually, she tried to please everyone and openly admitted that she feared disapproval. At times, she would say that she could not understand how anyone could like her, because she was not a very pleasant person to be with. At the author's suggestion, the group tried to determine what Pamela's "private goal" might be. Her history indicated that she was a girl who had always been "good" in order to be loved and appreciated by others, but that she inwardly felt that her efforts would be to no avail. Consequently, she felt "sorry for herself" and used both her friendly warmth and her self-criticism in order to continue feeling sorry for herself and induce others to sympathize with her.

Thereupon the group decided, "Let's all feel sorry for Pamela." The rest of the session was spent in commiserating with her and agreeing with all her self-critical comments. Pamela protested, blushed, grew anxious and said that this was not at all what she wanted. The group, catching on quickly, then expressed their sorrow that she was now suffering again; that is that she was being mistreated by the group. At this point, Pamela stopped talking.

At the next session, Pamela reported that she learned something. She said that she had been impressed by the previous session and had watched herself all week and caught herself looking for reasons to feel unhappy. She had then decided that she could find better ways of solving her problems. From that time on, a change in Pamela was apparent. She was seldom self-critical, but could be more critical of other members of the group, more objective in her evaluation, and had less need to please them. She dated her improvement from this point.

The presenting problem of Celia, an attractive girl in her middle twenties, was that she frequently fell in love with a new boy friend and used all her efforts to "make" him fall in love with her. As soon as the boy fell in love with her, she became tired of him and wanted to stop seeing him. Recognizing that her behavior was decreasing her chances of marriage, she came for therapy. In the group, she was reticent, did not speak at all about herself, would not show feelings and would not be "pinned down" by questions. She would answer a question with a question or would say, "I don't know." Some group members thought she was cold, others complained that they couldn't figure her out. Celia responded to the complaints by claiming innocence of any wrongdoing.

An analysis of Celia's life style showed that she viewed life as a continuous game of "one-upmanship." All human relations were competitive, and it was always important to remain the master of every situation. This she did in the group by admitting no defects and by avoiding any statements that might damage her position. She couldn't "come clean," because this would reveal her flaws and weaknesses, and then the others would be "one-up" on her.

Celia became more withdrawn at first after this exposure. The therapist suggested that the group award Celia a superior position by deferring to her on all matters. She was always to have the chair she wanted, all were to make complimentary remarks, and no topic was to be discussed without her acquiescence. These rules were generally adhered to for the rest of the meeting, though some of the more competitive group members could not comply with them easily. After several minutes, Celia "opened up" and described her problem. The group listened sympathetically.

At the next session, Celia, for the first time, brought in a dream (unrelated to the group). From that time on, she was more willing to expose herself and her feelings to the group. She answered questions, took sides in arguments and showed feelings more openly.

In one case, this technique was a conspicuous failure. Edith was an unmarried girl in her thirties, beautiful and intelligent. She was the only Negro in the group. Outside of her occupation, which she found very rewarding, she had almost no contacts with other human beings, leading an isolated life, feeling unappreciated and rejected. She always sat a little to the side of the group, closest to the door. She participated very little in the group conversations, except when the particular topic was one that interested her and then she would want the floor all to herself.

She was extremely critical of the others and was deliberately provocative, saying, "I want to see how they react to what I say." She never lost an argument—by the simple expedient of never accepting anyone else's logic. Her earliest recollections revealed the way in which she considered life and people unfair to her and in which she saw herself as a very special person who, while superior, was the victim of the envy of other people.

The group decided that Edith always wanted to be superior and special and wanted always to "have the floor"; and her chair was placed in the center of the group with the others sitting in a circle around her and all addressing all remarks to her. Edith closed her eyes and sat, abashed and annoyed. She said no word. In later sessions, there was no sign that the technique had in any way helped her.

A colleague, with whom the writer was discussing this technique, suggested a name for it.[2] He called it the "Midas technique" after the legend of King Midas, who had a lust for gold. Midas soon discovered that the ability to have all the gold he wanted was not the only desirable thing in life and decided that the "golden touch" was more curse than blessing.

The literature does not describe anything quite like the "Midas technique"; but the "auxiliary world" technique, described by Zerka Moreno[3] in a recent paper, resembles it in certain aspects. Here the group members and/or therapists act out roles which create for the patient the kind of world and kind of relationship he would like to have. This can be considered a form of confrontation.

Other authors have described techniques of confronting patients in group therapy. Wolf states:[4] "In the demonstration of a patient's provocative role the group is a natural and effective agent." Wolf described how group members can effectively help a patient to "discover his provocative role" by "dissecting" him. The Midas technique is also a way of "dissecting" the patient. However, it need not be hostile or humiliating to the patient.

Corsini,[5] discussing psychodrama in correctional institutions, mentions that a dramatic technique is often the only way of making a therapeutic impression on a difficult patient. Discussing a "defiant, contemptuous psychopathic adolescent," he says, "It was evident that he was well on the road to becoming a criminal . . . all the various forces and modes of communication that had been brought to bear on him had not [had] any effect. . . . The problem was how to impress on him the probable consequence of his behavior."

The use of the group to confront a patient with his behavior has also been described by Corsini in a discussion of analytic group psychotherapy.[6] He describes how a man with guilt about homosexual behavior and genital pruritis is confronted by other members of the group with the information that they know he wants to scratch his crotch and that they would prefer to have him scratch instead of fidgeting on the chair.

In addition to the promotion of "closeness" in the group—which he has previously described[1]—the author has been of the opinion that the chief value of this technique is that it permits the therapist to get an opening wedge into the patient's system of defenses and provocations; where analyzing and interpreting have only made the patient therapy-deaf because he could not translate the therapeutic situation into a meaningful experience. This seems one of the great items of value in group therapy, which is a "living" experience, as Ackerman[7] indicates.

Confronting a patient with his mistaken goals not only leads to greater spontaneity of behavior, insight and re-evaluation, but also promotes insight and re-evaluation in certain specific ways:

1. The patient is shown what his secret goal is.

2. He is shown that others are aware of his secret.

3. He is shown that it is acceptable to others and that they are even willing to help him achieve it.

4. However, by doing so, they indicate that what the patient has so greatly prized is not at all prized by the others. A thing that no one else wants tends to lose some of its value (as described by Papanek[8]).

5. The exposé spoils the "ploy." The group is "spitting in the patient's soup" by behaving in an unexpected way.

6. The ensuing acute awareness of the patient's behavior and the knowledge that the group is focused on it tend to inhibit such behavior.

7. The invitation to perform takes the steam out of the patient and further inhibits the behavior.

8. Unless the group can be seen as refusing the neurotic demand, it seems unimportant to work so hard for it. If it is so easily had, why worry about it? If the group is willing to give in, why fight for it?

After studying what had happened with Edith and why the technique had failed with her when it had been so useful in helping others, the following conclusions seem to apply: (a.) The technique and its purpose must be freely discussed and understood by the group members. (b.) The purpose must be to help a member, not to discipline or humiliate him. (c.) The atmosphere must be friendly. The group is engaged in giving a member something he secretly and/or unconsciously wants. It is not denying him or prohibiting him. (d.) Consequently, the patient must not be made to do something he doesn't want to do. Edith was forced to come to the center, while her behavior had shown that she wanted to be on the outskirts. Consequently, she felt forced by the group rather than freely accepted.

Furthermore: (e.) Whatever the private goal of the patient is, that must be what the group offers; whether it is sympathy, submission, admiration, etc. It is true that the group offers it in exaggerated form; this makes it all the more necessary for the focus to be correct. Thus, Edith's goal was not to be the successful superior being and the technique used was mistaken. In this case, the therapist and the group only saw Edith as trying to be superior and above; and did not see that it was much more likely that her private goal was to prove to everyone that she never could be accepted as she wished and that she would always be the victim of an unfair life. Thus, the faulty use of the technique only confirmed her pessimism. (f.) The group must genuinely be willing to accept the patient's private goal as if it were a legitimate demand on society and must feel free enough to have no need to control the patient. (g.) The Midas technique obviously requires a sense of humor on the part of the group. We are making fun of something a patient is doing (being careful not to make fun of the patient himself) and must do so with gentleness and friendliness.

REFERENCES

1. Shulman, Bernard H.: A psychodramatically oriented action technique in group psychotherapy. Group Psychother., XIII: 34-39, 1960.

2. Mosak, Harold H.: Personal communication.

3. Moreno, Zerka T.: A survey of psychodramatic techniques. Group Psychother., XII: 5-14, 1959.

4. Wolf, Alexander: The psychoanalysis of groups. Am. J. Psychother., III: 529-558, 1949.

5. Corsini, Raymond J.: Psychodrama with a psychopath. Group Psychother., XI: 33-39, 1958.

6. ——: Methods of Group Psychotherapy. P. 166. McGraw-Hill. New York. 1951.

7. Ackerman, N. S.: Psychoneurotic adults. In: The Practice of Group Therapy. S. R. Slavson, editor. Chapter 7. International Universities Press. New York. 1947.

8. Papanek, H.: Change of ethical values in group psychotherapy. Int. J. Group Psychother., XIII: 435-444, 1958.

CONFRONTATION TECHNIQUES IN ADLERIAN PSYCHOTHERAPY *

The characteristics and purposes of confrontation techniques have been variously described by different authors. Devereux (5), a psychoanalyst, perhaps the first to write on the subject, defines confrontation as "a device whereby the patient's attention is directed to the bare factual content of his actions or statements, or to a coincidence which he has perceived but has not, or professes to have not, registered." The purpose, says Devereux, is to "induce or force the patient to pay attention to something he has just said or done" in order to open up new avenues for examination and to increase awareness. Wolberg (17, p. 429) points out contradictions to the patient and asks him why he so behaved. He then examines the patient's response to the confrontation. Ruesch also uses confrontation to "confront the patient with the facts" and describes it as containing "an element of aggressiveness, and . . . designed to produce shock . . . usually demonstrates discrepancies between intent and effect, between word and action" (14, p. 194). Berne likewise defines confrontation as "pointing out an inconsistency" and suggests its use in three specific situations: when the patient tries to deceive the therapist, when the patient "plays stupid," or when he does not perceive the inconsistency himself (3, pp. 235-236).

Dreyfus and Nikelly describe the technique in existential language: "Two of the most important kinds of human relatedness which frequently occur during psychotherapy are encounter and confrontation . . . Confrontation involves being faced with a choice regarding one's existence. The therapist confronts the client with an aspect of the latter's world,

---

* Reprinted by permission from *Journal of Individual Psychology,* 1971, 27, 167-175.

and the client must choose whether or not he will respond and what the response must be" (7, pp. 18-19).

Garner (9, 10) more than anyone has described the various kinds of patient material on which confrontation may be focused. One may choose one of many "conflicts" as object of a direct, authoritarian statement, sometimes a command. No matter what the focus of the statement, Garner then adds, "What do you think or feel about what I told you?" (10, p. 24). The command is a message to the patient that the therapist is intervening and is therefore supportive. The question which follows "enables the therapist, by following the responses and behavior of the patient, to evaluate the degree to which doctrinal compliance or problem solving is developing in the patient" (10, p. 93).

All these authors tend to see confrontation as a direct challenge requiring an immediate response. Some use confrontation mostly to elicit new material, others, to increase awareness. Wolberg, and Dreyfus and Nikelly warn against making confrontations in such a way that the patient will perceive them as a hostile attack or a disregard of his feelings.

We understand by confrontation any reasonable therapeutic technique which brings the client face to face with an issue in a manner calculated to provoke an immediate response.

While Devereux carefully distinguishes between confrontation and interpretation, it is obvious from our definition that the two need not be mutually exclusive. Some confrontations are interpretations as well, but not all interpretations are confrontations. Thus, the statement, "Perhaps you arrange to suffer, so you can feel righteous," is an interpretation, not a confrontation, which the client may or may not accept. Even if it brings closure to him and satisfies his sense of fit, he is not required to do anything other than *consider* the therapist's comment. On the other hand, comments such as, "Why didn't you do it the way we had planned?" or "Why did you decide to stay and feel bad when you could have gone home?" are questions which request an immediate response, and thus are confrontations. Such questions can be made even more challenging by attacking the client's position, belief, or behavior, e.g., "Since you admitted that you provoked the argument, by what right do you still remain angry?"

The main characteristic of the confrontation is its *challenge,* and it is the combination of challenge and question which evokes the feeling that immediate response is required. "You behave with him the same way you behaved with your father," is an interpretation. But if one then adds, "Don't you?", the statement becomes an interpretation plus confrontation. The patient's response may be an explanation or a defensive maneuver, such as confusing the issues, changing the subject, or rationalizing (which maneuvers themselves become material for confrontation); or the response may be a positive therapeutic one in which the patient gains an insight, experiences a cognitive dissonance and changes a belief, or acts in a new way.

Confrontation is used to provoke therapeutic movement. As an active, directive technique it is less likely to be used by therapists who spend most of their time listening to free associations, being a "neutral screen," giving unconditional positive regard, permitting ventilation, or just offering emotional support. Action-oriented therapists, on the other hand, tend to use confrontation because it places the client constantly into new roles and situations to which he is asked to respond. Thus, Gestalt, experiential, sensitivity, and psychodrama therapists tend to move from one emotionally intense situation to another, with many confrontations (4, p. 16; 16, p. 92).

Group therapies by their nature contain numerous confrontations, because typically the members often confront each other (2, 11, 12, 13). Marriage and family counseling or therapy also lends itself to confrontations, as the family members are brought face to face with the dynamics of their relationships (14, 15).

A number of confrontation techniques have been used particularly in Adlerian psychotherapy. While Adlerian theory does not insist that the therapist be directive, it does say that the aim of therapy is to help the client recognize and change his mistaken goals and beliefs and their associated moods and actions. Such an understanding of therapy (which is very different from one of "working through" of inner conflicts) favors confrontation techniques since these are so effective in holding up before the client, as if in a mirror, his mistaken goals.

Of the following techniques some seem to be commonly used by Adlerians, while others have grown out of years of mutual endeavor of my more close Adlerian colleagues and myself. They are presented in terms of the object of the confrontation—the client's inner or overt behavior.

CONFRONTING THE CLIENT WITH HIS SUBJECTIVE VIEWS

Subjective Feeling

An agitated, distressed, unhappy young woman came into my office for her initial visit. Her description of her symptoms was not very clear, except that she feared having a "breakdown." But she made enough disparaging references to what her husband did or said that it was easy to guess that she was angry at him.

When she asked, "How sick do you think I am, doctor?", I responded with a statement intended to confront her with her emotions. "I'm not sure how sick you are," I said, "but one thing impresses me: you are very angry." The remark surprised her and she asked, "About what?" "From what I hear you saying, you seem to be angry at your husband. Am I right?" She immediately agreed, which allowed me to make an encouraging interpretive comment. "When people are very angry, they are also upset and they can even feel sick. So let us find out why you are angry at your husband and how much that anger may be upsetting you."

The patient later recalled this statement that she was angry, saying it gave her the feeling I was able to teach her something about herself.

Rudolf Dreikurs[2] gives the name, "revealing the hidden reason," to a confronting technique described in the following:

---

[2] Rudolf Dreikurs, personal communication.

The counselor had been discussing with a couple in marital counseling how each was out to "get" the other; he, by accusing her of fiscal recklessness; she, by excessive spending and complaints that his income was inadequate. At one session they each seemed to agree with the counselor's interpretations.

When they left his office, they passed a jewelry store, and the wife stopped to look in the window. Whereupon the husband said, "We were just talking about this in Dr. Dreikurs' office and here you go looking again at things to buy. Now, remember, you agreed to stop buying things." She immediately went in the store and bought a ring while he stood by protesting.

At the next session she was contrite, and he was triumphant. He offered the incident as evidence of her deficiences. She admitted that she had transgressed, and "could not understand" why she had done it.

The counselor asked, "What were you thinking at the moment you went in to buy the ring, just after your husband warned you?" At first she did not understand what the counselor was after, and said she did not recall. When asked, "What reason did you give yourself for going into the store?" she said, "I just wanted to go in and look at things. I had no idea of buying until I saw the ring, and it was so beautiful I just had to have it."

"What did you say to yourself then?" "I thought, now he was going to be angry with me again, but it was all his fault anyway. I had no intention of going into the store when I stopped to look in the window, but what he said made me so mad, I just said to myself that it was all his fault for always criticizing me even when I don't do anything, and that I was going to show him."

This was what the counselor was looking for, and he then said, "So you quietly wait until he says something that you consider provocative and then you use it to justify retaliation. In this way you can get him and make believe he deserved it."

"Hidden reason" describes the private justification and rationalization a person gives himself to make his behavior immediately acceptable to himself. Thus, "I'm only acting this way because I'm drunk," "I had so little sleep I couldn't get anything done if I went to work anyway," "I'm too nervous," are all examples of such private self-justifications. They give the person freedom from responsibility as Adler had observed. "Every therapeutic cure . . . tears the patient from the cradle of his freedom from responsibility" (1, p. 271).

Since this technique pinpoints a specific rationalization, it is not surprising that Albert Ellis also describes the same kind of pinpointing in his rational therapy (8, p. 126).

Mistaken Belief or Attitude

Since, for Adlerians, a person acts according to his convictions it becomes important to discover what are the convictions that have led to troublesome and distressing behavior. All material brought by the client is available for examination and for inferences regarding mistaken beliefs. But we are particularly interested in "basic convictions"; i.e., beliefs about one's own nature, the nature of the world in which one lives, and the nature of life, its meaning and requirements. These basic convictions fill in the following blanks: "I am. . . . Life is. . . . Therefore. . . ."

In Adler's words, a person's actions depend on the way he "looks upon himself and the world . . . Behavior springs from his opinion" (1, p. 182). "Each one organizes himself according to his personal view of things, and some views are more sound, some less sound" (p. 183). Those that are more sound, are in accordance with "common sense," those less sound, represent what Adler called at first "private map . . . for making one's way through life," the "private intelligence" (pp. 253-254), and sometimes also "private logic" (p. 143). Actually the last term is not quite correct, because even in patients the logic, the "therefore," is sound enough as a rule. It is their presuppositions, their opinions about themselves and life, which are not sound. Yet "private logic" has become the term preferred by Dreikurs (6, pp. 69, 96, 194, 271). But regardless of the term, the revelation of the patient's private beliefs is considered an important part of psychotherapy.

Showing the private logic. If the client who suffers from tension symptoms says, "Why am I so tense?" or, "How can

I stop being so tense?" or, "I never could relax, I'm the nervous type" or, "Wouldn't you be disturbed also?" or some similar form of verbal garbage that every therapist hears, the therapist can counter with an interpretation plus confrontation: "Since you see the world as inimical (hostile, dangerous, threatening), you must always be on the alert (keep your guard up, stay poised for action, keep your armies mobilized). Why should you expect to change the tension as long as you feel so surrounded by danger?"

Tua culpa. "Why do people walk over me?" asked another patient. "I'm only trying to be a good guy." The therapist's answer was, "Because you let them. You look, act and talk like a doormat, and you invite people to walk on you. Don't blame people, they're only giving you what you asked for. Since you invite them, you have to suffer the consequences. Isn't that right?"

The Private Goal

The private goal of the patient's behavior is often interpreted to him without confrontation, but there are common confronting techniques in this connection. One of these is the confronting interpretation which often elicits a "recognition reflex" (6, p. 261). Thus, when a patient tries to deny a feeling that the therapist suspects is present, the latter may say:

"Didn't you feel a little bit that you were glad he got upset?"

"Didn't you feel powerful, getting your mother to spend all that time with you?"

"Didn't you like all the fuss that was made over you?"

"Could it be you wanted to get your wife upset?"

"Didn't you think just a little that now you would have an excuse for staying home a little longer and not go to work yet?"

These types of confronting statements produce the recognition reflex more readily in children than in adults, but adults will also often respond with an indication that the remark hit home.

CONFRONTING THE CLIENT WITH HIS
DESTRUCTIVE BEHAVIOR

What Did You Just Do?

"Here and now" confrontations are considered by several writers (4, p. 16; 8, p. 126; 10) to be therapeutically the most active. While all confrontations mentioned have a quality of contemporaneity, those that deal with the immediate behavior of the client precisely at the moment of discussion are the most contemporaneous and simultaneous. They deal with his thoughts, feelings, and actions at the moment of questioning, often with his at-that-moment behavior in the therapeutic relationship, with his reactions to the therapy, especially his resistance, his repeated "game-playing," and his private logic.

For example, it is a common manifestation of resistance in intellectualizing, compulsive patients to respond to an interpretation by arguing about one word instead of dealing with the whole statement. One confronts this by simply saying, "I notice that you are arguing about one word. Why are you ignoring the rest of what I said?" Other manifestations of resistance can be confronted the same way. Some examples are:

"When I asked you about your parents you stopped talking. How come?"

"You just started to hallucinate. You decided to pay attention to the voices instead of to me. I wonder why?"

"You just changed the subject. Were we getting too close to something?"

"Whenever we talk about something important you belch. I wonder why?"

"Your face just turned red. What's up?"

Not only resistances, but other aspects of behavior can be noted:

"I notice you keep swinging your leg. What do you suppose it means?"

"A look passed over your face. What thought went through your mind?"

"How do you feel right now as we are talking?"

"The headache you are getting, started just a few minutes ago. What were we discussing then?"

"You just changed the subject again. Let's see if you can recall what the subject was when you chose to change it."

"Do you remember what I just said?"

"You just contradicted yourself. What are you trying to do?"

"You just made a slip of the tongue. Did you catch it?"

Especially useful are confronting statements which call attention to repeated patterns of self-defeating behavior.

"Now that you have told me your plans, I can see that you are planning to be a victim again. You still seem to insist on playing that role. Don't you?"

"You just berated yourself again. Keep it up and in five minutes you will really be depressed. Is that what you want?"

"You've spent the whole session complaining about your mother. I wonder when we can start talking about you?"

"Another married man? I think you are devoted to avoiding eligible men. And how do you expect this one to turn out?"

Presenting Alternatives

Confrontation is sometimes a dramatic way of presenting alternatives. This can be most clearly seen in role-playing where role reversal and auxiliary ego techniques provide immediate alternatives. In the dialogue situation one can confront with alternatives by statements like:

"You can study and try to pass the exam or you can goof off and pretend you don't care. Which will it be?"

"You don't have to spend your life complaining about how much your husband makes. You can get a job and help out. The choice is yours. Which will it be?"

"I know you don't want your in-laws to visit. You have three choices. You can tell them not to come; you can let them come and be gracious about it; or you can do what you did last time, let them come and spend the whole time being irritated and feeling abused. Which will it be?"

Examining the Future

Confrontation can also be used to present the future and its requirements to the client so that again, it is an immediate challenge, an attempt to evoke an immediate response.

Immediate future. Sometimes in the therapeutic dialogue a client recognizes the illogic of his behavior or a mistake in the way he thinks and feels. Sometimes he sees clearly the purpose of his symptoms and his behavior. At these moments the therapist may use confrontation: "O.K., you see it. What are you going to do about it?" "How long do you plan to wait before you change it? Six months? A year?"

Distant Future. Sometimes it is appropriate to confront the patient with a picture of the future in general and his life in it. For this purpose the following confronting statements can be used: "What do you plan to be doing five years from now?" "What do you intend to do with your life?" "What do you really expect to get out of all this therapy?"

Summary

Confrontation techniques are intended to challenge the client to give an immediate response, make an immediate change or an immediate examination of some issue. When appropriately timed they are effective additions to the therapist's armamentarium of techniques. They are *active* movements by the therapist, directing and guiding the attention of the client. Adlerian confronting techniques are intended to help the client become immediately and more intensively aware of his private logic, his goals, his behavior and his responsibilities for all these as well as his ability to change. Examples of the various confrontation techniques are given.

REFERENCES

1. Adler, A. *The Individual Psychology of Alfred Adler.* Ed. by H. L. & Rowena R. Ansbacher. New York: Basic Books, 1956.

2. Anderson, S. C. Effects of confrontation by high and low-functioning therapists on high and low-feeling clients. *J. counsel. Psychol.,* 1969, 16, 299-302.

3. Berne, E. *Principles of group treatment.* New York: Grove Press, 1966.

4. Corsini, R. J. Roleplaying in psychotherapy. Chicago, Ill.: Aldine, 1966.

5. Devereux, G. Some criteria for the timing of confrontations and interpretations. *Int. J. Psychoanal.,* 1951, 32, 19-24.

6. Dreikurs, R. *Psychodynamics, psychotherapy, and counseling.* Chicago, Ill.: Alfred Adler Institute, 1967.

7. Dreyfus, E. A., & Nikelly, A. G. Existential humanism in Adlerian psychotherapy. In A. G. Nikelly (Ed.), *Techniques for behavior change.* Springfield, Ill.: C. C. Thomas, 1971. Pp. 13-20.

8. Ellis, A. *Reason and emotion in psychotherapy.* New York: Lyle Stuart, 1962.

9. Garner, H. H. The confrontation problem-solving technique: developing a psychotherapeutic focus. *Amer. J. Psychother.,* 1970, 24, 27-48.

10. Garner, H. H. *Psychotherapy: confrontation problem-solving technique.* St. Louis, Mo.: W. H. Green, 1970.

11. Kaswan, J., & Love, L. R. Confrontation as a method of psychological intervention. *J. nerv. ment. Dis.,* 1969, 148, 224-237.

12. Lifton, W. M. Group centered counseling. In G. M. Gazda (Ed.), *Basic approaches to group psychotherapy and group counseling.* Springfield, Ill.: C. C. Thomas, 1968.

13. Mainard, W. A., et al. Confrontation vs. diversion in group therapy with chronic schizophrenics as measured by a "positive incident" criterion. *J. clin. Psychol.,* 1956, 21, 222-225.

14. Ruesch, J. *Therapeutic communication.* New York: Norton, 1961.

15. Satir, Virginia. *Conjoint family therapy.* Palo Alto, Calif.: Science & Behavior Books, 1967.

16. Shulman, B. H. The use of dramatic confrontation in group psychotherapy. *Psychiat. Quart.,* 1962, 36 (Suppl. Part I).

17. Wolberg, L. R. *The technique of psychotherapy.* 2nd ed. New York: Grune & Stratton, 1967.